Stepping Inside
The Story

Stepping Inside The Story

Sermons For Pentecost
(Last Third)
Cycle C First Lesson Texts

Thomas G. Rogers

CSS Publishing Company, Inc.
Lima, Ohio

STEPPING INSIDE THE STORY

Copyright © 1994 by
The CSS Publishing Company, Inc.
Lima, Ohio

All rights reserved. No part of this publication may be reproduced, stored in a retrieval system, or transmitted in any form or by any means, electronic, mechanical, photocopying, recording, or otherwise, without the prior permission of the publisher. Inquiries should be addressed to: The CSS Publishing Company, Inc., 517 South Main Street, P.O. Box 4503, Lima, Ohio 45802-4503.

Scripture quotations are from the *New Revised Standard Version of the Bible*, copyright 1989 by the Division of Christian Education of the National Council of the Churches of Christ in the USA. Used by permission.

Library of Congress Cataloging-in-Publication Data

Rogers, Thomas G., 1952-
   Stepping inside the story : sermons for Pentecost (last third) first lesson, cycle C / Thomas G. Rogers.
     p.   cm.
   ISBN 0-7880-0045-4
   1. Pentecost season—Sermons. 2. Bible. N.T. Gospels—Sermons. 3. Sermons, American. I. Title.
BV4300.5.R645   1994
252'.6—dc20   94-1001
                                                                                     CIP

This book is available in the following formats, listed by ISBN:
0-7880-0045-4 Book
0-7880-0046-2 IBM (3 1/2 and 5 1/4) computer disk
0-7880-0047-0 IBM book and disk package
0-7880-0048-9 Macintosh computer disk
0-7880-0049-7 Macintosh book and disk package

For Tricia

Table Of Contents

Preface	9

Proper 21
 Pentecost 19
 Ordinary Time 26
    Invest In The Future
    Jeremiah 32:1-3a, 6-15
	11

Proper 22
 Pentecost 20
 Ordinary Time 27
    Uplifted By The Blues
    Lamentations 1:1-6
	17

Proper 23
 Pentecost 21
 Ordinary Time 28
    An Unfamiliar Place For God
    Jeremiah 29:1, 4-7
	25

Proper 24
 Pentecost 22
 Ordinary Time 29
    Too Good To Be True
    Jeremiah 31:27-34
	35

Proper 25
 Pentecost 23
 Ordinary Time 30
    What Is God Doing In Our Bad Times?
    Joel 2:23-32
	43

All Saints' Sunday
    Whispers From A Dream
    Daniel 7:1-3, 15-18
	53

Proper 27   61
Pentecost 25
Ordinary Time 32
    The Pastor Who Created A Monster
    Haggai 1:15b—2:9

Proper 28   69
Pentecost 26
Ordinary Time 33
    Breaking Silence
    Isaiah 65:17-25

Thanksgiving Day   75
    There's More To Thanksgiving
    Deuteronomy 26:1-11

Christ The King   83
    Close Quarters With A King
    Jeremiah 23:1-6

Lectionary Preaching After Pentecost   91

C — Revised Common Lectionary; L — Lutheran Lectionary; RC — Roman Catholic Lectionary

Preface

During a church convention banquet I began talking to the man seated next to me. Before long the conversation turned to sermons. He asked me, "Why don't preachers tell more stories in their sermons?" He went on to say what a difference it made for him when his pastor told stories in the pulpit. He said, "Whenever I hear a 'regular sermon,' that is one without any stories in it, I feel like I'm a spectator watching the preacher build a house out of words. I sit there thinking of the preacher as a construction worker, building a house by stacking up information about God — one statement on top of another." He paused for a moment and then said, "I don't doubt that it's a perfectly fine house. I suppose that the structure is biblically and theologically sound, but the problem is," he said, "I feel like I'm watching it all at a distance."

Then his eyes widened and he said, "But it's different when there's a story involved. As soon as the preacher begins telling me a story, the distance between me and the sermon disappears. I find myself stepping *inside* the house." He said, "As soon as the preacher begins to tell a story I start listening more closely. I can't help myself. I don't know what it is, but I find myself leaning forward to hear because I want to know how it's all going to work out. It's like a little drama. When the preacher tells a story, I am no longer just a spectator observing at a distance. Suddenly, I'm inside the story with the preacher." The man stopped, looked at me with genuine confusion in his eyes and asked again, "So, why don't preachers tell more stories in their sermons?"

I mention this portion of my dinner conversation with this man because it helps describe the perspective from which the following sermons were written. I have prepared these sermons with the hope that they might be the kind of sermons that a hearer could "step inside." I suspect that my friend from the banquet might appreciate them. Each sermon uses "story" as an integral part of its design. The stories in these sermons are not used as sermon illustrations for making a "point," rather, the stories *are* the point. The intent is not to provide examples for ideas and information about the text, the intent is to draw the hearer into an experience of the drama that exists within the text.

For some of the sermons, I have focused on an engaging narrative of the biblical text itself. For the others I have created stories that are completely separate from the text and yet I offer them in the hope that they too can "draw us inside." To expand upon my banquet friend's analogy, we could say of this second group of sermons, that the goal is to step inside the house, but not necessarily to enter through the front door.

The drama of God's Word is not a story to be observed by spectators at a distance. God invites each of us to be full participants in this drama. It is my hope that the stories in these sermons may be preached and heard not simply as stories about someone else, but that God may grant us the grace to experience them as our own, once we step inside them.

Proper 21
Pentecost 19
Ordinary Time 26
Jeremiah 32:1-3a, 6-15

Invest In The Future

Cynthia stood before a church group in a neighboring town. She had been invited to share the story of her faith in her successful struggle against death. She stood before the group with a candle in one hand and a pocket lighter in the other.

She began, "Three years ago I went to the hospital for a series of tests and I was told that I had malignant cancer. I was also told that, although it was possible for me to take chemotherapy treatments, the chance of them offering any help at all was very slim. My doctors said treatments would most likely only bring misery to my final days. This was, of course, very bad news for me. I fell into a deep despair. I was ready to give up. All I could see was darkness.

"As I lay in this dark despair in my hospital bed, I started reading a Bible that was in my room. I happened to turn to the book of Jeremiah. What I read there changed my life. It also literally gave me life.

"In the darkest moment of my life, I read about the dark times that Jeremiah and the nation of Judah experienced. Following directions that he had received from God, Jeremiah prophesied for 12 years that Jerusalem would be destroyed. Finally, having angered the king by saying such things, Jeremiah was sitting in prison watching his prediction of doom come true. The Judean nation was on the brink of destruction. Her enemies were making their final assault upon the city. The Judeans who had already been killed lay unburied and those who were still alive suffered from famine and pestilence. The end was very near. Soon the enemy would break through and drag the survivors from their homeland into a captivity in a foreign land. It was a very dark time for them. As I read, it was easy for me to relate to the despair of their situation.

"In the midst of this hopeless and despairing situation, God led Jeremiah to do an incredibly hopeful thing. At the moment when things looked the worst, God led Jeremiah to purchase a field. He bought land in a country that was about to be taken over by the enemy. In this action Jeremiah was making an investment in the future. In the midst of a very bad time, he looked with hope to a better future of better times. Jeremiah knew that the hard times of exile were about to come upon the people of Judah, but God also led the prophet to symbolically proclaim that things would eventually get better and that God would return the people to their home. In faith Jeremiah saw that future. As a symbol of hope, he invested himself in that future by buying a piece of land."

Cynthia said, "When I read about Jeremiah's purchase of the field, it was as if God had suddenly brought a light into my darkness." At this point in her story Cynthia lit the candle she was holding. She continued, "I had a candle brought into my hospital room and I lit it that day as a sign of my hope — a sign that I was going to trust God like Jeremiah and invest in the future.

Cynthia continued, "Against the recommendation of my doctors I took chemotherapy treatments. In the process I got very sick and I came quite close to death. But, as I stand before you today, my cancer is in total remission." She raised the lit candle in front of her. "God gave me hope during my darkest times, during my bad times. Like Jeremiah, I put my faith in God and invested in the future. Now I praise God and celebrate the good times of health that the future has brought me."

At this point in her talk everyone in the group broke into spontaneous applause. Everyone, that is, except for a quiet man in the back row. After a moment he raised his hand and asked to speak. He said, "Your story sounds similar in many ways to a story that was a part of my life. It is very similar, but only up to a point. My wife also had cancer. She too had hope that God would move her through the dark times into better times. She invested in that future. She trusted God as the light to see her through her darkness. She took all kinds of treatments and she too got very sick. Together we hoped, together we prayed, and then she died." He said, "Please don't get me wrong. I am very glad that the future in which you invested turned out to have good times in it for you. But as you stand there holding that candle, I have to ask you — what do you think Jeremiah's hopeful action of purchasing a field has to say for my wife?"

All eyes were upon Cynthia. It was very quiet as they waited for her response. She also waited for her response, and then, discovering that she did not have one, told the man that she was sorry for his loss, blew out her candle, and sat down.

How are we to make sense of the man's question? Cynthia *did* understand this story correctly, didn't she? The purchase *is* a symbol of hope, is it not? The small plot of land that Jeremiah bought is a symbol of the whole land and the prophet is a symbol of all who will own property in the new age when Yahweh will restore the fortunes of Israel. Cynthia heard the story saying that we can make it through even the very worst times by focusing on the future — the time when God will finally set things right. Jeremiah's symbolic action seems to proclaim that there will be better times ahead. So, how do we respond to the man in the back row whose wife lit a candle in her darkness only to have it snuffed out by unsuccessful cancer treatments and finally by death? What can be said to the people who join Jeremiah in hoping for those better times, but then never experience any better times?

There is a definite tension in this story of the prophet's land purchase. The hopeful vision of a return to the land that Jeremiah's purchase symbolizes *does* turn out to be true. When we move ahead in the biblical narrative we learn that the exiles do eventually get to go home. Ironically, Jeremiah is dead by that time. And since the Lord had told him, "You shall not take a wife, nor shall you have sons or daughters" (16:1-2), his piece of land will pass on to others. For Jeremiah himself, the bad situation does not actually get better. He never gets to truly possess the land that he buys; he can only think about it and talk about it. The prophet invests in the future, but where does he *personally* reap the dividend? Is it perhaps even fair to say that, like the wife of the man in the back row, Jeremiah hoped for a light in the darkness, but that light was snuffed out before he had a chance to experience it?

As we struggle with some of these questions and tensions, let us consider the story of one more woman. Her name is Pamela. Pamela had a very rare eye disease. She was a very successful CPA in her mid-30s and she was going blind. Pamela tried everything. She went from doctor to doctor and they put her on special diets and gave her special treatments, but nothing seemed to stop the steady loss of vision. Finally an eye specialist told Pamela that she had one last option open to her. There was a very complicated surgery that could be performed. If it was successful she would be able to save some of her vision. If unsuccessful, she would go completely blind immediately rather than gradually with the natural progress of the disease. Pamela chose to have the surgery. She emerged from that operation with no sight at all and no hope for that to ever change.

Pamela's pastor went to see her in the hospital. The pastor took Pamela's hand and said, "I'm so sorry. Is there anything that you would like me to do for you?"

Pamela said, "Yes, there is."

The pastor said, "Just name it."

Pamela said, "I would like a candle."

The pastor was considerably surprised by the request, but said, "Fine, I'll be sure to bring one when I come next time."

Pamela said, "No. I want one now."

The pastor said, "Don't you even want to talk a little bit first?"

Pamela shot back, "If you really want to do something for me ...."

The pastor interrupted, "Okay. I see that it is important to you. I'll go get one right now."

It was a 15-minute drive back to church from the hospital, but the pastor made the round trip and returned to Pamela's room with a candle in hand. Approaching her bed the pastor asked, "Do you want me to light it for you?"

Pamela said, "Oh, no. Just hand it to me." She took the candle in her hands gripping it tightly. She then clutched the candle against her and said, "During these last months I have often thought of myself as a candle about to go out. I thought that everything I am is tied up in being able to see. I expected that when blackness came then there would be nothingness." She then said, "Now I'm blind. It's dark." She held the candle tightly. "But the candle is still here. I'm still here. I'm still me. God is still God. It's going to be okay somehow."

Perhaps in her blindness Pamela was able to see something in her candle that eluded Cynthia when she held up her lit candle before the group. Cynthia saw the flame of her candle as a symbol of hope. The flame was the symbol of light in darkness — God helping us out of bad situations. This can be a powerful symbol for people who have passed through darkness on the way to better times. But it did not speak to the man in the back row. And there may be times when this will not speak to us either.

Pamela, however, experienced the candle in a different way. She discovered that a candle is more than a fragile light. Flames come and go on candles. But, as Pamela discovered, a flame doesn't make a candle. It's the candle itself that makes a candle a candle. For her, the candle proper was a symbol of hope, because, regardless of whether there is a flame or not, her hope came in the promise of candleness itself. She came to realize that hope is not grounded in *what* will happen to us, but in *who* we are.

Each of us have our own terrible times. You know what yours have been. Perhaps you are in the middle of some pretty bad times right now. Yet, when things go badly for us that is not a time to despair, but a time to invest ourselves in the future.

When Jeremiah bought the plot of land, he invested in the future. In the middle of terrible times he made a symbolic purchase — a statement of hope grounded in God. Yet, ultimately, Judah's hope did not rest in whether or not good things would happen to them, but in who they were, a people grounded in a covenant with their God. Yes, the land was an important issue, but its importance lay in the fact that it was a part of the covenant promise. Their hope came not in *what* would happen to them, but in *who* God had made them to be — a people of the covenant.

We, like Jeremiah, are called to invest in the future. We do so not because we are certain that God has something better in store for us, but because we know *who* God has made us to be. Like Pamela, we can think of ourselves as a candle. We have good times and we have bad times. The flame may come and the flame may go. Ultimately it does not matter. Our hope is not grounded in the promise of good things happening to us. Our hope is grounded in the fact that we have become children of God.

The hope we receive from God is not a promise of a constant and steady flame that will take away all the dark times. Our hope comes in the promise of candleness itself. Our hope comes at the core of who our God has created us to be. We are a people washed in the waters of divine forgiveness and acceptance. We are a people who live in and live through the church — a community based in love and service and justice. That is the very essence of who we are. Our identity is in Jesus Christ and his church. That is the core of who we are. That is our candleness.

That means that even in the worst of times we can invest in the future, for in the love of Jesus Christ, God has invested everything in us.

Proper 22
Pentecost 20
Ordinary Time 27
Lamentations 1:1-6

Uplifted By The Blues

Raymond looked down at the pages of the open Bible in front of him. What he saw was a rather eerie sight and it sent a slight shudder through his body. All the words on the pages were covered with blue marker. Six months earlier Ryamond himself had carefully highlighted every single word on these pages with a light blue marking pen. At the time that he had marked the pages he had no expectation of ever turning to those pages of his Bible again. Now, to his own amazement, he found that he had once again opened his Bible to this strange book — one that he had colored solid blue from the first verse to the last. What book was it that gave a visible shudder to this middle-aged man? Raymond's Bible was open to the book of Lamentations. But before any of this can make very much sense to anyone, we need to back up a bit in the story.

Six months earlier things appeared to be going fairly well for Raymond. In fact, a casual observer might even have looked at Raymond with a bit of envy. Raymond was a very upbeat guy who consistently looked on the bright side of things. He was married and had three children of high school and college ages. Raymond had a good job as an accountant with a large firm. He and his wife were good friends with a number of couples. And to top it all off, Raymond was a committed Christian who worshipped every Sunday and read his Bible regularly.

It is with Raymond's Bible reading that the story really begins. You see, Raymond not only read his Bible regularly, he read it carefully. Having worked as an accountant for a number of years, Raymond had developed a very exacting way of looking at things. Raymond saw things in a very "cut and dried" manner. The balance of an account was clearly either positive or negative — in the black or in the red. There was never any question. Upon reflection, Raymond realized that part of the reason why he liked accounting was that it was always easy to distinguish good news from bad news. Everything was always either black or red. As an accountant, he never had to deal with balances that were dark red or charcoal red or black with just a shade of red. It was a mathematical enterprise. Everything was always positive or negative. There was no middle ground. The precision of numbers had a great appeal for Raymond.

To have such an exacting view of things was a wonderful asset when doing accounting. However, when it came to reading his Bible, Raymond frequently got frustrated, Raymond read his Bible because he wanted to be uplifted by God's Word. Yet sometimes Raymond got frustrated. As he began to read his Bible, he could never tell in advance whether he was about to encounter something wonderfully uplifting or something horribly depressing.

For example, Raymond once turned to the book of Psalms. His pastor had frequently mentioned that the book of Psalms was filled with inspirational prayers. Raymond opened his Bible and began reading Psalm 138. There he read, "I give you thanks, O Lord, with my whole heart; before the gods I sing your praise." He continued, "On the day I called, you answered me, you increased my strength of soul" (Psalm 138:1, 3). Raymond liked what he had read. It lifted his spirits. "The pastor was right," Raymond thought to himself. "This is a very upbeat part of the Bible." Raymond decided to read more. He glanced to the verse immediately preceding the verses he had just read. As he read, Raymond's uplifted feeling did an about face. The words he read were a cry for revenge by Israel against her enemies. He read, "Happy shall they be who take your little ones and dash them against the rock!" (Psalm 137:9). Whoa! Raymond had not seen that one coming. A gruesome image began to form in his mind involving blood-stained rocks and small, limp bodies. Suddenly, and without warning, his supposedly uplifting Bible reading time had become very depressing.

Raymond considered the problem before him as if it were a math equation to be solved. He read his Bible in order to be uplifted — not to become depressed. It was frustrating not to know in advance what he would encounter as he read. In his accounting he could distinguish the positive figures from the negative ones at a glance. The so-called black and red balances were clearly indicated. Yet with his Bible he had no clear indication what was positive and what was not. He had no option other than to read the passage, and then, if it *was* depressing, it was too late.

It was at this point that Raymond decided, in a very good accounting fashion, to color code his Bible. He chose a very simple system. Whenever he read a sentence that made him sad or depressed, he highlighted it with a blue marker. Any parts that were uplifting and joyful he marked in yellow. All the rest, anything that was not particularly depressing or uplifting, he left blank. Blue for the "blues." A bright sunshine yellow for the cheery parts. Raymond was confident that once he had done this he would never be caught off guard by a particularly depressing verse. In fact, he could avoid them altogether.

Now it would perhaps come as no surprise to anyone that, since Raymond was a very exacting person, he began his project in a very methodical way. He started at the very first page of his Bible and worked his way through book by book. As he read, Raymond discovered that every book of the Bible contained a combination of passages that both uplifted and depressed him. Each book was a complex mixture. As a result, every one of the first 24 books of Raymond's Bible had a smattering of both blue and yellow markings when he had finished reading them. There were no exceptions. None. That is, not until he came to the 25th book — the book of Lamentations.

As Raymond read the book of Lamentations, he thought it was *the* most depressing thing he had ever encountered. It consisted of page after page of grief and despair over the destruction of Israel. There was no plot. Most of the chapters were acrostics — poems in which each verse begins with the next letter of the alphabet in order. Most chapters had 22 verses, the number of letters in the Hebrew alphabet. Every verse presented an image of mourning and grief. Apparently the intent was to create a thoroughly tragic feeling — despair from A to Z. This was exactly the kind of book that Raymond was eager to avoid. *Every* single sentence received his blue verdict. Not only was it all depressing, it was depressing *poetry!*

People like Raymond, people who have a very exacting way of viewing life, often have a fairly minimal appreciation for the value of poetry. Raymond had always avoided poetry. He was a person who loved the "this is exactly what it means" character of accounting. By comparison, Raymond considered poetry, with its many possible interpretations, to be a very inefficient way to communicate. Raymond thought it was amazing that Lamentations was even in the Bible. It was depressing *and* it was poetry. He made a mental note to avoid it like the plague.

Raymond's first encounter with Lamentations was six months ago. Shortly afterward, Raymond began to feel that he was the victim of another kind of plague — in fact, a series of them. To begin with, his wife left him for another man. She told Raymond that she needed to be with someone who had more passion in his life. Shortly after his wife had filed for divorce, Raymond learned that he had not received a promotion that he had been expecting. The job was given to someone younger, someone who had spent a fewer number of years with the firm. During this same period of time Raymond also noted that his children seemed more and more distant from him. Their own lives were very full and it seemed that they had less and less need for him. He sensed that they made subtle efforts to avoid him.

Everything seemed to crash in on Raymond at once. He was devastated by loneliness and failure. He felt that he had failed as a husband and father. He also realized that he had probably advanced as far as he would ever advance in his work, which wasn't nearly as far as he had imagined for himself. A mid-life crisis and the loss of his family combined to make Raymond one very miserable person. He turned to his friends for comfort and support. They all agreed that it was tough to go through a divorce, but many of them were divorced themselves and considered it a pretty standard part of life. From their point of view Raymond still had it pretty good. They reminded him that he had his health and a good job and they told him that his kids were just going through a stage. The comfort that Raymond received from his friends was pretty minimal and generic. He spoke and then they spoke, but there was no real hearing and no comfort in the words. Raymond tried to explain to his friends how desperate he really felt, but he could not seem to find the words, and they did not really seem to have the time.

Raymond slowly began to discover that his friends had not really been *his* friends at all, but rather they were friendly couples who had been friends with Raymond and his wife. Now that Raymond was only half a couple, the friendships that had been formed between pairs became strained and finally ended in polite, and eventually permanent, avoidance. Raymond was deep in grief, but there was no one around to notice.

If Raymond ever needed some uplifting it was now. Fortunately he knew exactly where the uplifting passages were in his Bible. Raymond read one joyful, yellow verse after another, but nothing spoke to him. He read about God's glory and goodness. He read all about healing and hope, sprinkled generously with "hallelujahs," but he seemed to be reading it all from a great distance. He might as well have been on another planet. Raymond felt alone and empty and afraid.

This is the place that we found Raymond when we began. In his own depression and discouragement Raymond turned to the blue verses. In fact, he had opened his Bible to the woeful, solid blue book of Lamentations — a place to which he had planned never to return. As he looked down at the pages of poetry covered in blue, a slight shudder ran through him.

He read aloud, "How lonely sits the city that once was full of people! How like a widow she has become, she that was great among the nations." As he read something happened to him. Raymond did not understand *why* it was happening, but he knew that it *was* happening — he was being drawn into the poem. Raymond knew that he was not a widow. He knew that the poem was not talking about him. Nonetheless, the grief that this widow felt spoke to his own grief. As someone who had always avoided poetry, Raymond did not know that authentic poetry could bring a unique human feeling to life in the heart of the reader.

Raymond read on, "She weeps bitterly in the night, with tears on her cheeks; among all her lovers she has no one to comfort her." Deep inside himself Raymond knew something about bitter night and he whispered aloud to himself, "She has no one to comfort her." Raymond was no longer reading the poem. These were his words. This blue book of poems had provided Raymond with inspired words that spoke for him when he could not find adequate words of his own.

Raymond had been pulled into the poem and into the story that it told. Raymond was not, of course, an Israelite in Babylon grieving the destruction of his homeland. Nevertheless, Raymond was with those people in their story. He was with them in their pain and loss. The voice of their lament gave voice to his own pain and loss. Their story of suffering was his story. Someone understood. And to his utter amazement, Raymond found the whole experience . . . uplifting.

Raymond read the entire book of Lamentations. He embraced the story as it reached out to embrace him. When he had finished the book of blue poems Raymond kept on reading. Reading now from *within* the story he turned also to passages that he had marked earlier with his bright yellow marker. He read from Isaiah, "Sing for joy, O heavens, and exult, O earth; break forth, O mountains, into singing! For the Lord has *comforted* his people, and will have compassion on his suffering ones" (Isaiah 49:13). He read the words of Paul, "Blessed be the God and Father of our Lord Jesus Christ, the Father of mercies and the God of all consolation, who consoles us in all our affliction" (2 Corinthians 1:3-4). The words of comfort no longer seemed foreign to Raymond. He had entered the world of the story of God's people. His pain was still present, but he also experienced God's offer of comfort and hope in the midst of that pain.

The next day was a Sunday. As usual, Raymond went to church. There, Raymond made another discovery. The same kind of tensions that he had found in his Bible were also present in the experience of worship. As he sat in his pew, Raymond had an awareness of the blues and yellows blending together in what was happening. At the altar the pastor prepared the table for the eucharist, the meal of thanksgiving and joy. It was a meal of victory, forgiveness and salvation. Yet Raymond listened closely to the words that surrounded this meal of joy. The pastor spoke of Christ being broken. Jesus was giving his blood, blood that had leaked out of holes that had been torn in his body. Jesus was also giving his body, flesh that had been stretched and cut and ripped. It was a scene filled with intense pain. Yet it was here that Raymond met a loving and forgiving God. Earlier, Raymond had felt that he had no one to comfort him. Here, in this meal of painful joy, Raymond felt the presence of someone who would comfort him. In the strange blue and yellow world of worship Raymond was uplifted.

When Raymond got home from worship that Sunday, he again took out his Bible and his colored markers. He turned to the solid blue, depressing pages of Lamentations. Raymond took the cap off his yellow marker and began to move it across the words. The bright, sunshine yellow mixed with the "blues." Raymond had discovered that there is indeed a deep and powerful joy that can only be experienced out of the depths of sadness and pain. Raymond had come to realize that even the depressing book of Lamentations plays an important role in God's Word. As Raymond moved the joyful, yellow marker across the trails of blue, a new color emerged. As Raymond observed it he decided that it was a good color for the Word of God. Deep within the emerging green on the pages before him Raymond sensed the mysterious blending of suffering and comfort in the life of God's people. Through God's grace Raymond had discovered a new color for God's Word. It was the color for new life.

Proper 23
Pentecost 21
Ordinary Time 28
Jeremiah 29:1, 4-7

An Unfamiliar Place For God

They looked over their shoulders one final time to see what was left of their city and their homes. The prisoners searched the rubble with their eyes hoping to find a familiar sight. They longed to see something familiar that might bring comfort to their unsettled hearts and minds. But when the smoke from the fires cleared enough for them to see, they saw only empty spaces where their houses had stood. They felt anger toward the soldiers who had replaced their homes with sky, but their anger turned to sheer pain as they saw the agonizing emptiness that replaced the building that had been the center of their lives. In angry disbelief they stared at the empty space where Yahweh's temple had previously stood. This look was their last visual memory of what had been their home and their religion. As their captors led them over a hill, the city dropped out of the prisoners' sight. The citizens of Jerusalem were then led to Babylon. They were led into exile.

I suppose it is possible to say that once the exiles got to Babylon they experienced a kind of peace. Yes, technically the fighting was over. Still, it would be pretty hard to imagine that they had much of an inner peace or much peace of mind. Try to think how you would feel. Suddenly, you are in a totally new environment. Everything is unfamiliar, uncomfortable and unsettling. How could a person find a real peace — the settled feeling that comes from the comfort of being surrounded by that which is familiar?

The exiles naturally longed to return home where things were familiar, comfortable and settled. So what did they do? I suppose you could say they did what many prisoners do. They "did time." They waited. Oh, they continued to go through the motions of living, but they had their hearts and minds on hold. Things would not really be okay for them until they got back home. Hopefully it would be soon. They had heard rumors that some of the prophets, like Hananiah, were saying that the return would take place *very* soon.

Then the letter came. One of Yahweh's prophets, Jeremiah, wrote to the exiles in Babylon. We can envision the scene. The people gather around to hear the letter read. It is a moment of hopeful anticipation. Maybe the kind of peace for which they are longing is just around the corner. Hopefully Jeremiah has a message from Yahweh that says they will quickly return to Jerusalem and get away from this strange place and their hated Babylonian captors.

They open the letter and begin to read. What they hear is nothing short of shocking. In fact, the first thing that shocks them is what they do *not* hear. For us to get the full impact of this letter we need to understand that letters during this period always began with a salutation that included some expression for "peace." The writer would say something like, "Shalom. Peace to you" or "Peace to you and your family." We see the same kind of thing in Paul's letters in the New Testament that begin, "Grace to you and *peace* from God ...." To the exiles' surprise, Jeremiah includes absolutely *no* polite salutation. He rudely and abruptly jumps right in and tells the exiles to get to work. After he has given them instructions, for what they are to do, *then,* in v. 7, comes the deferred word of peace. "(The Lord says) Seek the welfare (shalom) of the city where I have sent you into exile." In other words, Jeremiah's letter says that if they are looking for a normal word of peace — forget it. They need to do their work first. Once their work was done, *then* they would hear the word of peace. And what is the work they are to do?

Jeremiah says they are to build and plant and raise families. They are to settle in as full-fledged members of the community. They are to quit thinking of themselves as prisoners of war. They are no longer simply to "do time." Through Jeremiah's letter Yahweh tells them that they are not in Babylon accidentally. They are not just the victims of bad luck. They are not to spend their days moping for Jerusalem and the good ole days. They are not to shirk away from their captors, hating them as their enemies. Rather the exiles are to reach out to the Babylonians in good will. They are to work for the welfare of the land. They are even told to pray for the land and its people. They are to seek "shalom" for their captors. They are to pray for *Babylon's* welfare and peace. God tells them that in Babylon's peace the Israelites will find their own peace.

This was *some* letter! It was revolutionary, to say the least! These exiled Jews had always been a people set apart from others. In their seclusion they found their peace with God by making sacrifices in the temple in Jerusalem. Now the sacrifices were gone. The temple was gone. Jerusalem was gone. In this crazy letter God seemed to be telling the people to get ready to meet God in a new way — in places and people that for the exiles would be unfamiliar, uncomfortable and unsettling. In this amazing letter God was telling the exiles that they would find peace in places and people that they would never have expected. As amazing as it seemed, Yahweh was telling them that if they were looking to Jerusalem for their contact with God, they would be looking in the wrong place.

This 29th chapter of the book of Jeremiah tells a very interesting story in Bible history. Jeremiah's brief letter is a truly revolutionary message from God. This is, without a doubt, one of the most amazing moments in biblical history. And *perhaps* it is even more than that. When we read this passage we encounter a very intriguing question: Is it possible that this story is *more* than just a history lesson? Could it be that when we read this passage we are reading an ancient letter through which God is still actively speaking to people? Could we be those people?

There are some questions which we should probably ask ourselves: Is the experience of the exiles really that different from our own? Do we not sometimes find ourselves in a changing, complex and difficult environment that occasionally feels like a foreign land to us? Don't we, like the exiles, earnestly search for peace of mind? Don't we at times experience places and people that are unfamiliar, uncomfortable and unsettling to us?

If we are honest, we probably have to answer "yes." We do long for the same kind of peace that the exiles wanted — a settled feeling that comes with the comfort of the familiar. When we encounter situations that are unfamiliar, uncomfortable and unsettling for us, we may long for a return to the way things used to be — more familiar, more comfortable and more settled. When we encounter people who are to us unfamiliar, uncomfortable and unsettling, we may long to separate ourselves from them and surround ourselves with vague carbon copies of ourselves; we are confronted, at times, by those who are *not* like us.

Poor people may be uncomfortable around wealthy people and vice versa. Some people may wish to avoid those with different customs than their own. The young may resist the old ways as strongly as the old shy away from the young. Physically challenged persons may seek to avoid people who seem "too perfect" while they are themselves avoided by many. Some may be uncomfortable with those of a different race or sexual orientation. Many people may wish to avoid those who would hurt them — not only physically, but with words or by rejection or by simply ignoring them.

At this point you might be wondering where this preacher is going with all this. Surely there is nothing wrong with our seeking peace of mind by placing ourselves in the company of people with whom we are comfortable. It certainly doesn't seem that striving for comfort in this way would be such a terrible thing. True enough, it doesn't *seem* like it would be. Yet there is still the matter of Jeremiah's letter before us. What if it *is* more than just a history lesson? What if Jeremiah's letter is speaking a challenge to us that is equally as revolutionary as it was to the exiles?

If that is the case, Jeremiah's letter totally turns things around. God tells the exiles, "You are looking for peace in a completely wrong place." Is it possible that God is saying the same thing to us? God tells the exiles to look for peace in the land of their enemies. God tells them to look for peace in a place that for them is: unfamiliar, uncomfortable and unsettling. Is it possible that God is saying the same thing to us? The Bible doesn't tell us the exiles' response, but Jeremiah's letter was no doubt a real shocker. They must have looked at each other with wide eyes thinking, "This is unbelievable, incredible, beyond understanding."

If we consider that this letter might be a message to us, do we have the same response as the exiles? Is the whole concept just as unbelievable, incredible or beyond understanding today as it was over two millennia ago? Is it possible that sometimes we look for peace in the wrong spot? Do we look for God in the wrong place? Could God actually expect us to find peace by consciously moving into places and relationships that are strange and uncomfortable? Could God really want us to purposefully associate with those who cause us not only discomfort, but even pain? Does God truly expect us to make an effort to reach out to those who have hurt us in some way — the ones who come closest to receiving the label of "enemies"?

It's one thing to turn the other cheek, as it were. It is one thing to resist doing something to actively harm an enemy. But to seek them out and actively promote their welfare — that's really pushing this! This just doesn't make a lot of sense. That is beyond understanding. That is simply beyond all understanding!

We cry out to Jeremiah, "It's okay for you to write revolutionary letters to the ancient exiles. It's okay to ask them to do a complete 180-degree turn to find God and whatever strange peace God intends for them. It's really no problem for you to have asked them, long ago, to embrace the unfamiliar, the uncomfortable and the unsettling. After all, they are all dead and gone now. But, Jeremiah, do you seriously expect us to think that God could still be speaking through you to us now? Seriously, isn't that a bit much? In fact, it's pretty close to unbelievable. Let's make sure we've got this right. Are you asking us, by our own volition, to move into caring relationships with people who make us feel uncomfortable? Are you saying that doing that will give us peace? We just can't understand that kind of logic. It is simply beyond understanding."

We cry out to Jeremiah and it's God who responds. God says to us, "You're right. It is all quite beyond your understanding. It certainly is." God responds to us through another inspired writer. Through the apostle Paul, God sends yet another revolutionary letter — this one is addressed to the Christians at Philippi. The letter says, "The Peace of God, which passes all understanding, will keep your hearts and minds in Christ Jesus." "Yes," God says, "the kind of peace that I have in mind for you does pass understanding. It passes *all* understanding." God goes on to say we will have this peace when our hearts and minds are "in Christ Jesus." And what does that mean? Think about it. If our hearts and minds are in Christ Jesus, where will that lead us? Just where do we find this Christ Jesus?

Well, a good look at scripture's record of Jesus' life shows us that Jesus seemed to take God's revolutionary command in Jeremiah's letter quite seriously. Jesus did not seek out only those who were like him and who liked him. Instead, he also actively sought out those who did not have much love for him. He even reached out to those who were his enemies, those who did him harm. Jesus also reached out to the kind of people who might make some of us feel uncomfortable. He entered into relationships with lepers, marginal members of society, sick people, criminals, unscrupulous tax collectors and pathetic prostitutes.

In a word, Jesus embraced sinners. The perfect, sinless Son of God became a prisoner in a strange and unsettling world filled with sinners. But rather than just "doing time" and counting the days until he again would be at home in heaven with the Creator, Jesus got to work. He reached out to those who dwelt in the foreign land of sin in which he found himself. And for that we should be most grateful. For, in that act of intentionally reaching out to sinners, Jesus entered into a relationship with each of us. He became our loving friend. It is this very story of his love for us that unites us together as we gather for this worship. The one who knew no sin reached out to the likes of us. He did it consciously and with great love. The whole thing must have been unfamiliar, uncomfortable and unsettling to him. But, thank God, he did it. We rejoice in his loving actions that drew our lives to his. We call it: the good news. We could also call it: the good example.

We, like the exiles who first received Jeremiah's letter, are understandably looking for a word of peace. God's word to us is the same word that the exiles received: Get to work. Reach out actively and in love both to those who are easy to like because they are like us *and* to those who are unfamiliar, uncomfortable and unsettling to us. It is *there* that we will find the peace that is promised. For the promise is true. The peace of God, which passes all understanding, will keep your hearts and minds *in* Christ Jesus. And it is always *there,* in the unfamiliar, the uncomfortable and the unsettling, that we will find this Christ.

Proper 24
Pentecost 22
Ordinary Time 29
Jeremiah 31:27-34

Too Good
To Be True

Jim was 16 years old. He'd only been driving for six months, but already his parents had paid the fines for two tickets that Jim had received for speeding. On the day that Jim's parents received a notice from their insurance company telling them that the cost of their automobile policy had been increased, they told Jim that they needed to talk. After supper, Jim and his parents sat at the kitchen table. It was a serious gathering.

His mother began, "We seem to have a problem here. We know you want to be able to drive the car and we want you to be able to. But you need to understand how important it is to obey the speed limits."

Jim's father spoke. "Your mother and I have talked about this and we have agreed to allow you to continue to use the car *if* you agree not to speed again." The father looked directly at his son, "Are you willing to agree to that, Jim?"

Jim said, "Yes."

His mother handed him a sheet of paper. She said, "We thought this was important enough to put in writing so that it was absolutely clear to everyone." Jim read the two sentences on the paper in front of him. "We agree to let Jim use our car." Below this sentence both of Jim's parents had signed their names. The second sentence said, "I agree not to break any speed limits while driving the car." Below this sentence there was a blank line for Jim's name. Jim signed the agreement.

Two weeks later Jim got another speeding ticket.

Jim's parents were upset and disappointed. They had attempted to make a serious agreement with their son, but it had not worked. The big question was: What would they do now?

In some ways the story of the agreement between Jim and his parents is similar to the scene described in today's Old Testament lesson. A very important agreement, a covenant, had been made between God and the people of Israel. Yahweh had promised to be their God and care for them while the people had promised to live according to the commandments that God had given them at Mount Sinai. In Old Testament times the making of covenant agreements was a serious business. We know this both from biblical sources and from records of some non-biblical covenants that have survived from that period.

Covenant making was surrounded with ceremony. The promises were made before witnesses. The documents recording the agreement were placed in a special place and provisions were made for periodic public readings. The promises that each party made were *not* to be taken lightly. For example, the Hebrew phrase "to make a covenant" literally means "to *cut* a covenant." When covenants were made there was actually cutting involved. To signify the seriousness of the covenant pledges, a number of animals were each cut into two parts and the parts were separated. The participants in the covenant then walked between the parts of the animals as a symbolic way of saying, "If I do not keep my promises in this covenant, may what has happened to these animals happen to me." Covenants were literally made in blood. The book of Exodus describes some of the ceremony that was involved when the covenant at Sinai was "cut." We read, "Moses took the blood (from the sacrificed oxen) and threw it on the people, and said, 'See the blood of the covenant that the Lord has made with you' " (24:8).

With a full awareness of just how serious it was, the children of Israel entered a covenant with Yahweh at Mount Sinai.

They promised to obey the commandments that God had written on the tablets of stone for them. They promised to follow the moral guidelines found there.

Then, just like 16-year-old Jim did, the people of Israel broke their promise. Many times in the book of Jeremiah Yahweh speaks through the prophet describing the way in which the people were ignoring the covenant. In chapter 7 of Jeremiah the Lord says, "This command I gave them, 'Obey my voice, and I will be your God, and you shall be my people; and walk only in the way that I command you, so that it may be well with you.' Yet they did not obey or incline their ear, but, in the stubbornness of their evil will, they walked in their own counsels" (7:23-24). Again, in chapter 11 the Lord says, "They did not obey ... but everyone walked in the stubbornness of an evil will. So I brought upon them all the words of this covenant, which I commanded them to do, but they did not" (11:8). Finally, in our text for today, chapter 31, the Lord refers to this Sinai covenant as "a covenant that they *broke,* though I was their husband." The Lord uses the analogy of a broken marriage. The people had broken their promise. They had broken the agreement.

In other passages of the book, Jeremiah goes to great lengths to let his readers know that Yahweh was upset and disappointed. God had attempted to make a serious agreement with the people, but it had not worked. The big question was: What would God do now?

But first, let's return to Jim's house. Jim's parents thought and thought about what they should do. The parenting books that they had read recommended that the best thing to do would be to let their son experience the logical consequences of his actions. At the same time, Jim's parents knew how important the car was to their son and they hated to see him go through the agony of being denied the use of it. The two of them talked about it for a very long time. What should they do?

Finally they came to a decision. They called Jim to the kitchen table. It was another serious gathering. Jim realized that he had blown it big time. He knew that only a miracle could save him now.

Jim's father held the signed agreement in his hands. Without saying a word, he held up the sheet of paper in front of him and tore it in two. Then he looked at Jim and said, "This agreement did not work. Your mother and I have decided to make a *new* agreement with you. We're not going to write this one down, so please listen closely, Jim."

Jim needed no encouragement. He was already listening very closely.

His father said, "The *new* agreement is this: We agree to let you use our car and you agree not to break any speed limits while driving the car."

Jim stared at his parents. He was confused. What he had just heard his father say sounded exactly like the agreement his father had just ripped up. Jim said, "I don't get it. What is *new* in the new agreement? What is different from the first agreement?"

Jim's mom responded, "We love you, Jim. We love you more than you can probably ever know. We believe that you are a good kid. We are going to forget about your previous speeding tickets. We are going to pay the fine on this new one and then we are going to forget about it too."

She gave her husband a quick glance and continued. "What makes this a *new* agreement is that we believe that you will keep your promise this time. You messed up and we have forgiven you. We hope that, in the process, you have come to a better understanding of how much we love you. We expect that it will make a difference in how you view your relationship with us. We expect that you will keep this new agreement with us not because you are *supposed* to, but because you *want* to."

Jim sat in disbelief. They were not only giving him the use of the car, they were giving him their unconditional love and forgiveness. It was too good to be true.

Again, the story of the agreement between Jim and his parents is quite similar to the story of the covenant between Yahweh and the people of Israel. As we have already noted, the people had completely broken their covenant promises and God was upset. They had blown it big time. Only a miracle could save them now. That miracle was to be found in the free forgiveness of God.

Some Bible scholars refer to our text as the most important passage in all of Jeremiah and one of the mountain peaks of the entire Old Testament. It begins with these words, "The days are surely coming, says the Lord, when I will make a new covenant with the house of Israel" (31:31). Talking to a people who do not deserve it, God says, "I love you." God makes them a promise. "The days are surely coming," says the Lord," when I will make (that is, I will "cut") a new covenant." God planned to cut *this* covenant differently in order to show God's great love for the people.

"The days are surely coming," writes the prophet and, sure enough, the days of this new covenant did come. In Jesus Christ God entered into the world of time and space to cut a new kind of covenant with God's people. In this new covenant, it was not animals that were to be sacrificed and cut. It was the Christ himself who was cut. On the Friday, which we call "Good," it was *his* blood that flowed.

Looking further at our text, it appears as if God expected that the proclamation of a new covenant that was centered in God's love and forgiveness would bring about a change in the people. Earlier in the book of Jeremiah God had spoken with anger against the people saying that their sin "is written with an iron pen; with a diamond point it is engraved on the tablet of their hearts" (17:1). What a different message in our text for today! The Lord says, "I will put my law within them, and I will write it on their hearts; and I will be their God, and they shall be my people" (31:33). God now says that instead of sin, God's law will be written in the people's hearts. For something to be written on a person's heart is a Hebrew expression that refers to the person's character. The heart is understood to be the seat of decision making.

Notice what is being said here. The new covenant does not involve the giving of new law. That is unnecessary. The people had already received God's law in the first covenant at

Sinai. The only real difference between the old covenant and the new is that this time the people will be faithful. "I will be their God, and *they shall be my people.*" God seems to expect that, in response to God's forgiving love to the people, they will begin to obey the law. They will do so not because they are *supposed* to, but because they *want* to. It will be written on their hearts. It will be so deeply a part of their consciousness that it will become a part of who they are. Incredible! It was too good to be true!

As you can see, the two stories in this sermon are similar in many ways. Both Jim's parents and God loved their children. They offered them forgiveness. As a result, Jim and Israel became new people. A new agreement, a new covenant, was created. Who would have thought that love could have such a power to change people? It was amazing! It was too good to be true!

Yes, that is exactly correct. It *was* too good to be true. After the *new* agreement went into effect Jim did okay for a while, but then he was pulled over for doing 72 in a 35 MPH zone. It turned out to be a mixed bag for the children of Israel too. They had their moments of faithful obedience, but they also continued to break and ignore the laws that were supposedly now written on their hearts.

At Jim's house, his parents took the car keys from him. They had paid Jim's other fines because he had complained of having no money of his own. For this final speeding ticket his parents sold Jim's stereo and Nintendo and used the money to pay the fine.

There are probably some of you who, as you hear what Jim's parents did, are mentally applauding them for finally doing some responsible parenting. You may well be thinking that Jim was long overdue for some "tough love."

God, on the other hand, may not get much applause in the parenting department. God does not resort to strong discipline. In Jeremiah God promises to "remember their sin no more" and then in the New Testament we encounter the climax of this promise in the death of Christ as an atonement for people's sins. God pays the price for our sin. God pays the fine for our breaking of the law.

What's going on here? Does God have really lousy parenting skills? Did an all-knowing God really expect that people would magically change in response to this crazy kind of new covenant? Was God actually surprised when people did not begin to lead completely pure and moral lives in response to a lavish display of love and forgiveness? How could that be? We know God is not stupid. What's going on here?

For this text to make sense we need to return to the beginning of our sermon text. The first words are: "Behold the days are coming." This is an eschatological formula. In other words, this is a phrase that Bible writers use when they are referring to future events. Once we know this, it gives a whole new perspective to the passage. The complete fulfillment of the new covenant of which God speaks will only come into existence at the end of time in the world to come. Until then, it serves as a metaphor. It is a vision from God of what our covenant relationship with God will *some*day become. At that time we will perfectly become the people God created us to be. It is a glorious vision, but for now, it is too good to be completely true.

Even though it is only a vision of the future, it is nonetheless an important part of our Christian walk on this side of eternity. The Christian faith has always acknowledged that the kingdom of God is a paradox. The kingdom will not come into full splendor until the second coming and, at the same time, the kingdom has already begun in the coming of Christ. Our new covenant with our God in that kingdom hangs in the tension of being "already but not yet."

As a result, we are a lot like Jim and the children of Israel. Sometimes we do pretty well. Sometimes we live and act in a way that it appears that God's law is indeed written on our hearts. Perhaps there are even times when what Paul said of the Corinthians could be said of you, "that you are a letter of Christ ... written not with ink but with the Spirit of the living God, not on tablets of stone but on tablets of human hearts" (2 Corinthians 3:3).

At other times, we do a very poor job of keeping God's law. We blow it big time. I know those times in my life. You know those times in your life. Yet, when it happens, God does not give up on us. God continues to look at us through "behold the days are surely coming" eyes. God is a parent who knows that a new day *is* coming when the children will finally live lives of complete love and service to one another.

Until then, we each have our good moments and our bad. And in the midst of it all we have God's incredible promise in this text: "I will forgive their iniquity, and remember their sin no more" (31:34). The promise of the new covenant is not a promise that we will become sinless, but rather, it is the promise for the forgiveness of our sins.

It is the same promise that we experience each time we celebrate the eucharist. It is the promise we receive along with the bread and cup. The cup of promise that Christ offers us is the new covenant in his blood, which is given and shed for the forgiveness of our sins.

What a joy it is to receive such an incredible outpouring of love from our God! What a powerful love it is that we experience! It touches and changes us. We become new people. A new reality is created. It's as though God's vision of the new covenant becomes more than just a vision. In the midst of such joy we think, "This is too good to be true!" And then ... another reality sets in and we find ourselves sinning once again. We think sadly to ourselves, "Yes, it *is* too good to be true."

That is finally where we always end up, isn't it? The whole vision of a new covenant in which we *always* stay connected to God is just that — a vision. The idea is just *too* good to be true. That's where it all ends ... except for one last thing. It would all end there except for the fact that our God does, in fact, have some pretty strange parenting skills. God continues to look beyond our sin, no matter how many times we mess up. God continues to reach out to us, to love us and to forgive us no matter how many times our sin angers and disappoints God. God promises to be a heavenly parent who will *never* leave us to pay the fine ourselves when we break the law. We ask ourselves if it is really possible to have such a parent? Well, such a thing would definitely be *too* good to be true, except for the incredible good news that it *is* true.

Proper 25
Pentecost 23
Ordinary Time 30
Joel 2:23-32

What Is God Doing In Our Bad Times?

When Frank and Karen got home from their Bible study at church, there were two messages waiting for them on their telephone answering machine. Both messages were bad news. One call was from Ted, one of Frank's friends at work. Ted had received tragic news about a death. The other call was from Paula, one of Karen's friends from her aerobics class. Paula had received tragic news from her doctor. Neither Ted nor Paula were actively involved in a church. In the past, Frank had invited Ted to church and Bible study, and Karen had invited Paula, but both Ted and Paula had declined the invitations. Neither of them thought about God very much — at least, not until tonight. Now, God was suddenly very much on both Ted's and Paula's minds. Neither of them knew of a pastor to call, so Ted had called Frank and Paula had called Karen. Both phone calls were desperate pleas for help.

Ted's message was first. "Frank, this is Ted from the office. I'm sorry to bother you like this, but my wife and I got a phone call this evening." Ted's voice began to break up. "Our son, who lives in Germany, was killed in a car wreck." There was a long pause before he could continue. "I just don't know what to do. I don't know what to think." There was another pause and the sound of muffled sobs. Ted continued, "Frank, I know you are always reading the Bible and all that. I thought maybe

I could talk to you. I hope it's okay for me to be calling you like this, Frank, I just don't know what's happening. Why would God let something like this happen? What is God doing?" There was another pause while Ted tried to collect himself. "I guess I've changed my mind about reading the Bible with you. If you could come over for a little bit, I'd sure appreciate it. We couldn't get a flight until tomorrow morning, so I'll be at home all night. If you can, please bring your Bible and come over.

There was a beep and Paula's message followed on the tape. She was sobbing. "Karen, this is Paula. Oh God, I wish you were there. I hate talking to these machines. Karen, I really need to talk to you. I didn't tell you yesterday at class, but my doctor was running some tests on me because she suspected a problem." Paula began to sob harder. "Karen, I just found out that I've got bone cancer. It's bad." There was a pause while Paula tried to collect herself. "I didn't know who else to call. I'm so scared. I need some help here, Karen. I know we don't really know each other that well, but you're the only person I know who even talks about God. Karen, I don't know what's going on. Why is this happening to me? What is God doing?" Paula took a deep breath. "I *really* hate these machines. God, I wish you were there. Please call me when you get in. Better yet, come over if you can. Please."

Both Frank and Karen picked up their Bibles again and headed back out the door. It was a bad time for each of their friends. With Bibles in hand, Frank and Karen set out in different directions to try to answer the same question. In the midst of their respective suffering and confusion, both Ted and Paula had asked the same question: "What is God doing?"

When Frank reached Ted's house, Ted was alone. His wife had gone over to her sister's house. The two men sat at the kitchen table to talk. After they had talked for a while, Ted looked down at Frank's Bible lying on the table. Ted knew that Frank had been to his Bible study that evening. He asked Frank, "What did you study about tonight?" Then, he added with a hopeful tone, "Was it anything that applies to me?"

Frank said, "Our church group has been studying the Old Testament prophets. This evening we looked at the book of Joel." Frank gazed down at the Bible in front of him and thought for a moment. Then, looking up at Ted, he said, "Joel is probably a good book for you right now. It talks about why bad things happen and what God wants people to do."

Ted listened as Frank described the events recorded by the prophet Joel. Frank explained that there was a terrible plague of locusts that swept across the land of Israel. The locusts came in wave after wave after wave. All the crops were destroyed and the people had nothing to eat. They were devastated. It was a *very* bad time for them. The prophet told the people that the terrible thing that had happened was not just a coincidence. The locusts were God's army and they were sent because the people were not worshipping properly. They had turned away from God. The prophet told the elders and all the inhabitants of the land that they must fast and cry out to God. The prophet said, "Return to the Lord, your God." The people listened to what the prophet was telling them and they prayed to God. God then answered their prayer and blessed them.

Frank looked at Ted and said, "Think of your son's death like the locust plague. Even though it is devastating, you can see that, in a way, it is a good thing. God is using it as a way to get your attention — a way of letting you know that you have not been worshipping properly. Just like in the book of Joel, God is giving you a message. It's the same message: 'Return to the Lord, your God.' You wanted to know what God is doing. That is what God is doing."

Frank was just about to ask Ted if he wanted to pray, but he saw that Ted was standing up. As Frank looked, he saw that Ted was trembling. Frank could not tell if he was trembling with anger or illness. Actually, it was a combination.

Ted spoke slowly in a very restrained voice, "Frank, I know I asked you to come over here, but now I am going to have to ask you to leave. I cannot listen to any more of this. You're telling me that the Bible says God intentionally took my son's life in order to *punish* me? If I were to believe that what you are saying is true, I would die myself from despair. But before I did, I would use my last breath to curse a God who would do such a thing! Please go now. Please leave and take your Bible and your God with you!"

When Frank had gone, Ted sat at the table with his head in his hands. He cried long into the night. He felt so alone in his pain. There was an aching emptiness deep within him. He had hoped that somewhere there was a God who could fill that emptiness. Ted knew now that that would never happen.

Meanwhile, in another part of town, Karen arrived at Paula's house. Paula was also alone. She was divorced and had no children. At first, Karen just held her friend and let her cry. Eventually Paula stopped crying and the two women went into the kitchen and made some coffee. As they sat at the kitchen table, Paula looked at Karen and said, "Please tell me. What is God doing?"

Karen had, of course, attended the same Bible study that evening as her husband. Like Frank, Karen's mind jumped immediately to the book of Joel. After thinking for a moment, Karen, just as her husband Frank had done with Ted, decided that the message from the prophet Joel was a good way to explain to her devastated friend what God was doing.

Karen opened her Bible. She told Paula that the prophet begins by describing a great plague of locusts. Karen said that the reason for beginning with the devastation of the locusts and famine was to show that no matter how great a problem is, God is greater still.

Karen and Paula began to read together at the verse in Joel that begins today's Old Testament lesson. In the midst of the devastation that has passed through the land, God tells the people to "be glad and rejoice in the Lord your God" (2:23). Karen said there was reason to rejoice because of the promises that God made to the people.

First, God promised that there would be plenty of rain so that "the threshing floors would be full of grain," and the vats for the wine and oil would "overflow" (2:24). Before, the locusts had been eating everything. Now the focus is on the people eating from the abundance of what God will provide. God promises to meet the people's needs in the midst of their devastation.

Karen read the next verse. God says, "I will *repay* you for the years that the swarming locust has eaten" (2:25). Karen remembered what she had learned in the Bible study earlier that night. Karen explained to Paula how, in Hebrew, the word for "repay" used here also has the meaning of "healing" or "making whole." God is sensitive to the total loss that the people have experienced. God knows that the ordeal has left psychological scars far deeper than only the direct effects of the famine. There is a God who thoroughly understands people's pain.

The two women continued reading. God says, "I will pour my spirit on all flesh" (2:28). Karen explained that before this time God's spirit had only come to a select few — special leaders and some prophets. Moses had said that he wished "that all the Lord's people were prophets, and the Lord would put his spirit on them!" (Numbers 11:29). Now it was happening, *everyone* received the spirit — old and young, the men and the women, the slaves and the free. Karen looked up at Paula and said, "Actually, God was talking only about the Hebrew people. It was *their* sons and *their* daughters referred to here. But later on, on the day of Pentecost, Peter quotes these very verses as the spirit of Christ was poured out on all people indiscriminately." Karen smiled at her friend, "You and I are included in this."

Karen said, "The same God who made all these promises to a people who were in the middle of a very bad time, is the same God who is with you now in your pain and suffering. God is in the midst of those who suffer. God promises *not* to leave you alone."

After they had talked a bit more, Karen gave Paula another hug and went home. Even after Karen had gone, Paula found herself crying softly to herself. Her tears were different than the tears that Ted was crying across town. Paula's tears were tears of joy. She was still afraid, but she no longer felt so alone. Deep within her an empty space had been filled by a gracious, loving and understanding God. It was a God she had met in the book of Joel.

Obviously Karen's visit had a happier ending than Frank's, but who was right? Both Ted and Paula had a devastating thing happen to them. They each asked what God was doing. Were they, as Frank had suggested, receiving God's punishment for what they had done? Or were they, as Karen had suggested, receiving God's presence for what they were going through? Both Frank and Karen were basing their statements on scripture. In fact, they were quoting from the same book. Who was right?

There is a popular phrase that you sometimes see on bumper stickers. "The Bible says it. I believe it. That settles it." It sounds simple. The problem is that it is not always that simple. What do we do when the Bible seems to say conflicting things?

For example, the Old Testament prophets proclaimed a message based on a commonly held belief of their time: The bad things that happen to people are God's punishment for their having done wrong. Book after book in the Old Testament proceeds from this assumption. But, not *all* Old Testament books agree with this assumption. Job is a good example of an Old Testament book that strongly disagrees with the assumption. In fact, one of the main themes of the book of Job, if not *the* main theme, is that the popular "do wrong, get clobbered" understanding is incorrect. The premise of the book of Job is that suffering comes to a person who has done *nothing* wrong. The book of Job flies in the face of the assumption made by the prophets.

The disagreement on this principle continues into the New Testament. When Jesus and his disciples meet a man blind from birth, the disciples ask Jesus, "Rabbi, who sinned, this man or his parent, that he was born blind?" (John 9:2). They automatically assume that this problem is a punishment for someone having done wrong. Jesus, however, completely ignores the disciples' question and shifts the attention from the *cause* and focuses on how this is an opportunity for a loving God to *act*. When Jesus sees other sick and miserable people he does not give them a lecture on how their sin has caused their problems. No, Jesus simply reaches out to them with healing hands of love and compassion. Just as God was in the midst of devastated Israel, Jesus stands in the midst of people devastated by all manner of hurts and suffering.

We need to be very careful when we ask whether Frank or Karen was right in their interpretation of Joel. Not only is this an important question, but it may also lead some to ask an even deeper question. The deeper question is this: If the Bible does, in fact, seem to say conflicting things, is the *whole* Bible true? The answer to this question is a clear "Yes." The Bible *is* the bearer of God's revealed truth. Having said that, we need to also remind ourselves that the Bible is also a complex book composed of many different kinds of literature. It is perhaps helpful to see the similarity between the Bible and an anthology that would be used in a world literature class. The anthology might include ancient Greek tragedies, Renaissance novels, 18th century European poetry, and 20th century American short stories, just to name a few of the categories. It is all "good literature," but each of the works are also very, very different from one another. A student should be careful not to read an ancient Greek tragedy with the same expectations one would bring to a 20th century American short story. The reader needs to be aware that belief systems and writing conventions differ from century to century and from genre to genre.

The Bible is very much like an anthology. When we read the book of Joel, we need to read it for what it is. It is itself a complex mixture. It includes classic Old Testament prophecy, which assumes that God does indeed punish bad deeds. Some scholars suggest that it also borders on being apocalyptic literature that looks to the future using symbolic language.

Perhaps the best method for unraveling the puzzle that is the Bible is to follow a guideline that Christians have used for centuries. We need to recognize that, in early times, God's relationship to God's people was understood in certain ways, but Christ's coming brought with it a new perspective for reading God's Word. In our study of the Bible we seek to understand what a book like Joel meant to its original hearers. Then we also ask what it can mean to God's people today. It is possible that these two meanings will not always be exactly the same. For example, let's consider the passage in Joel that discusses the pouring out of God's spirit. Like so many other Old Testament promises, this passage bursts its original wrappings and leaps into the New Testament with wider and deeper significance. Now the words of this ancient prophet refer to the pouring out of the Spirit of the crucified and resurrected Christ. When we read the book of Joel today, it is certainly God's revealed truth, but it is a truth that we see through the lens of God's ultimate revelation through Jesus.

It would be so good if Ted could come to know that. It would be so good if this parent of a dead son was not separated from God precisely at the time when he needs God's presence and comfort the most.

When anyone, Christian or otherwise, is mourning the death of a loved one, that is simply *not* a time to quote Old Testament passages dealing with punishment. It is not the time to say, "God is giving you this to test you, to make you stronger." It is not the time for "We cannot understand why God did this, but you must accept it. It is God's will." No. No. No. It is not the time for *any* of that.

When people in the middle of their bad times ask what God is doing, it is a time to gently reach out to them in their devastation and remind them of the good news of God's presence which is revealed in Jesus. In the midst of bad times the good news needs to be spoken and it needs to be spoken clearly. God does not *create* our suffering. God *shares* our suffering. God says, "When you hurt, I cry with you. I share your pain." Our God is a God who can say to Ted and his wife, "I too know what it is like to have a child die."

This is not only good advice for what to tell others. It is also precisely what we ourselves need to hear. No doubt, some of you here today have devastation in your lives right now. For some it may be relatively small. For others, not small at all. Some are probably worried about money, others about health. Some of you may be experiencing hurt in your relationships with family members or others whom you care about. Some may have experienced the loss of someone or something that you loved a great deal. Some of you may have something in your life that makes you afraid. Whatever kind of devastation there may be in your life this day, the good news promises of the book of Joel are for *you*. God says, "I promise *not* to leave you alone." God's words through this prophet ring true through the centuries. Whatever your need is this day, these words are true for you. God promises, "I am in your midst ... know that I, the Lord, am your God."

All Saints' Sunday
Daniel 7:1-3, 15-18

Whispers From A Dream

As Tishra rocked her young son, it was all she could do to hold back her tears. She thought back to her earliest memory of God. As a young girl she heard the rabbi read the story of creation from the holy scroll. She learned that, in the very beginning, God made all the world and the world that God made was good. As a child, Tishra experienced a world that had indeed seemed good to her. It was a secure world. She prayed daily with her family and each week they observed the Sabbath. The world into which her son had been born was different. It was not the same secure world of Tishra's youth.

Now, as an adult, Tishra was very conscious of another story — the one that followed the story of the creation of a good world. It was the story of the first sin and the "fall" of the good world. Sin changed everything. The goodness of God's creation was invaded by evil. As a Jew, living in Jerusalem during the reign of Antiochus IV, Tishra had encountered a very vivid, first hand experience of evil.

Ten years earlier, Tishra's family, and all of Jerusalem, had come under the rule of one of the cruelest tyrant kings of all time. His name was Antiochus IV, but he gave himself the name "Epiphanes," which means "manifestation." The king believed that the Olympian god Zeus was manifest in him. However, this arch villain was anything but a god. In secret,

...s subjects called him not Epiphanes, but "Epimanes," which means "madman." He was mad with power. He used his power cruelly for his own purposes and gave no thought to the pain he caused.

For example, the ritual of sacrifice by the Jerusalem temple priests, especially by the high priest, was the sacred center of life for Tishra and her husband, Moshi. This was true for all of the faithful in Jerusalem. But Antiochus Epiphanes had no care for the people of Jerusalem and no reverence for the temple sacrifices. For him, the whole thing was nothing more than a financial opportunity. When the evil king came into power, he removed the current high priest and offered the job to the highest bidder. To the dismay of the faithful Jews, the man who won the appointment to be high priest proceeded to sell the gold furnishings from the temple to pay for his purchased position.

As Tishra continued to rock her child, she thought back on how she and Moshi had been appalled at the thought of what Antiochus had done and what he had allowed to be done. It was truly appalling, but it was only the beginning of what this evil king would do. Some years passed and then the evil reign of Antiochus reached a nightmare level for the Jerusalem Jews. Tishra remembered it all with agonizing clarity. She had been pregnant with her son at the time. Antiochus had been on his way to attack Egypt when he received an order from Rome calling off the attack. The command from Rome put the king in a bad mood. So, on his way home, as he passed near Jerusalem, Antiochus decided to wipe out the city and colonize it with Greeks. Tishra and Moshi watched in horror as 20,000 soldiers entered the city. They plundered what was left of the temple and attacked the men. The plan was to kill all the men so that no army could be assembled to resist them.

The most hideous part of it all was that Antiochus attacked the Jews on the sabbath. Sabbath observance prohibited the Jews from protecting themselves by fighting back against their attackers. Panic and terror seized Tishra and Moshi. In the street outside their home they heard screams as the Jewish men, their friends and neighbors, were killed in cold blood by the king's soldiers. In desperation Moshi hid in a trunk in their bedroom. The soldiers burst into the house, but they did not look in the trunk. Once it grew dark, Moshi escaped into the night. Shortly afterward he joined a resistance army led by Judas Maccabaeus.

Antiochus was brutal in his attack upon Jerusalem. His army did great damage to the city; they enslaved the women and children; and they killed every Jewish man who had not been able to escape. Even with all this, still greater evil was to come. Antiochus had a garrison built and the city was occupied by the king's troops. Then, King Antiochus Epiphanes issued an edict. All the people in his realm, including the Jews, were to observe the same religion. They were to worship at the altar of Zeus. The king even placed an altar for sacrificing to Zeus in the Jewish temple. The edict proclaimed that anyone who refused to comply would do so on pain of death.

As Tishra rocked her son, she remembered how horrible the news of the edict had been. If ever she and the others longed for the comfort that came to them through worship, it was then, in their grief and loss. Even though the king's appointee remained as high priest, any opportunity for the people to worship the true God was nonexistent.

Rocking her son, Tishra recalled the pain of childbirth and the even greater agony that came with bringing a child into such a world. The king's fanaticism was without parallel. He had robbed the Jews of everything that had true importance to them: the Torah, their sacrifices, their food laws. Everything that bore the mark of traditional Judaism was uprooted — gone.

As Tishra held her son, tears she had been trying to hold back finally began to run down her face. She was thinking now of the crowning blow of the king's evil edict. The "madman" had even prevented her from having her son circumcised! Her son was not permitted to receive the mark of the people's covenant with God. This evil king had indeed taken *everything* from them! The anguish welled up within Tishra.

Her silent tears turned to sobbing. The child in her arms sensed that something was wrong and he began to cry with her.

It was in this moment of fearfully deep despair that Tishra remembered the dream. God's prophet, Daniel, had had a dream, a vision. Through a secret underground network of communication the prophet's dream had been whispered from Jew to Jew. Out of the depth of her despair Tishra remembered the words that had been whispered into her ear. The prophet's dream was a dream about the evil Antiochus, the king who had robbed them of so much. He had even robbed them of hope and a meaning for their lives. The dream openly acknowledged all the horrendous evil that the people had suffered and continued to suffer under this "madman." Then came this promise: "*But* the holy ones of the Most High shall receive the kingdom and possess the kingdom forever — forever and ever" (Daniel 7:18).

Tishra had learned from the Rabbi that she lived in a "fallen world." The experience of rampant evil in this fallen world was horrible for Tishra. It drove her to the depths of despair, and it was *there*, in the pain and agony of her despair, that she recalled the wonderful, whispered word from the prophet: "BUT." The message of the dream was clear. Yes, the evil of this king is great, "BUT" there is more that God would have you know. Evil rules now, "*But* the holy ones of the Most High (God's people) shall receive the kingdom and possess the kingdom forever — forever and ever.

Tishra returned to the message of the dream again and again in her mind. She thought to herself, "The past had been terrible. The present is terrible. *BUT*, God has control of the future." As Tishra held her child to her, she rocked him with a new perspective on her situation. Tears still ran down her face, but there was hope in her eyes again. In the dream that God had given the prophet she saw enough of the future to hold firm. "Things are bad, *BUT* . . ." "*BUT* . . ." In that single word Tishra heard good news. In that word she found hope.

Miles away, Tishra's husband, Moshi, was also deep in despair. He desperately missed his wife and the son he had never seen. Things did not look good for the resistance fighters. The strength of the evil king's forces far outweighed their own. There was reasonable cause for despair. However, Moshi had also heard the hushed whispers of Daniel's dream. He knew that the evil Antiochus had great power and threatened Moshi's very life, "BUT ..." Yes, it looked as if they would probably lose the upcoming battle, "BUT," the dream brought the promise that they would win the war. The prophet's dream involved both the present *and* the future. Evil rules now, *"But the holy ones of the Most High (God's people, God's saints) shall receive the kingdom and possess the kingdom forever — forever and ever."*

Like it had for his wife, the prophet's dream also gave Moshi a new perspective on his situation. He saw enough of the future to give *meaning* to his fight. They might lose the battle, "BUT," God had already announced who would win the war. "Things are bad, *BUT* ..." "*BUT* ..." In that single word Moshi heard good news. In that word he found meaning for his struggle. Even if he were to die, he knew that his death would have meaning.

Finally, on December 14, 164 B.C.E., an amazing thing happened. Judas Maccabaeus' band of resistance fighters successfully defeated the alien forces. The temple was cleansed and the lights in the temple were lit. The event is still remembered and celebrated by Jews today in the festival of Hanukkah. It was a happy ending to a long ordeal!

One might wonder if this victory of the Jews brought an end to the useful life of the message that is couched in Daniel's dream. Daniel's dream was a gift of promise to the Jews who lived during the evil reign of Antiochus. Was Daniel's prophecy intended as a Word of God only for the people of that time? I believe the answer is "No." The message through the prophet's dream most certainly *was* directed to people who were living under the evil oppression of Antiochus Epiphanes, but it is by no means limited only to God's "holy ones," who lived in the second century B.C.E. Daniel's dream is a message from God that continues to be whispered in the ears of

God's saints, the ones God makes holy. This message continues to be a vitally important message for all the saints. Daniel is also speaking to us.

Like Tishra and Moshi, we too live in a "fallen world." We may not battle evil in the form of a ruler like Antiochus Epiphanes, but we certainly battle evil in a myriad of other forms. We struggle against injustice, cruelty, violence, apathy and abuse. We battle the evil of a fallen creation that manifests itself in broken health — in injury, sickness and death.

Even in the 20th century, it is still quite easy for God's saints to get overwhelmed. Pastors' offices are frequented by saints who are depressed and filled with despair. Many others do not discuss their pain with their pastor or others. They choose to suffer silently, but they suffer nonetheless.

It is quite understandable that God's present day saints would, on occasion, experience despair — in fact, deep despair. It has always been difficult for God's people to live in a fallen world. As much as any of God's saints ever needed the promise, we also have a need to hear the promise of Daniel's dream whispered in our ear. Yes, there are genuine reasons in this present age for us to despair. *"But* the holy ones of the Most High shall receive the kingdom and possess the kingdom forever — forever and ever." In the prophet's dream we hear the distant echoes of still other promises that scripture makes concerning the future of God's holy ones. In Matthew's gospel God promises that we "will see the Son of Man coming on the clouds of heaven with power and great glory. And he will send out his angels with a loud trumpet call, and they will gather his elect" (Matthew 24:30-31). In the revelation given to John we hear of a future in which the saints will *finally* move beyond a "fallen world." The day is coming when there will be "a new heaven and a new earth." For God's saints there is the promise of a future in which God "will wipe every tear from their eyes. Death will be no more; mourning and crying and pain will be no more" (Revelation 21:1, 4). Yes, things are difficult now, *"But ..."*

In the thick of the struggle with evil in a fallen world, you, as one of God's saints, may not *feel* victorious. However, for God's saints, it is not a matter of how you *feel;* rather, it is a matter of what you *know.* The words of Daniel's dream also catch up the spirit of God's promises surrounding Christ's return. These words have been whispered again in your ear this day. Daniel's dream is intended to give you a new perspective on things. Your existence in a fallen world may well be filled with causes for genuine despair. Even so, you can know that what you experience now is only a chapter in a much larger story. The good news is that the ending of the story has already been whispered to you through a prophet's dream.

Be careful not to underestimate the power and importance of this dream. In our day and age the word "dreamer" is often used in a rather derogatory sense to describe someone whose head is lost in the clouds — an idealist out of touch with reality. In the prophet Daniel God's saints experience quite a different kind of dreamer. This "dreamer," this one with "visions in his head," is a true visionary. He is the one who can see beyond appearance to reality. He sees beyond events to ultimate meaning. This dreamer moves God's saints of every age beyond the happenings of history to the realization of God's triumphant future. Yes, evil is rampant now. *"But* the holy ones of the Most High (God's saints) shall receive the kingdom and possess the kingdom forever — forever and ever." Let all God's saints hear the message of *this* dream.

To whatever extent you may be experiencing depression and despair this day, listen to the whispers of this dream. Listen to this dream with an open heart and mind. God is whispering to all the saints. God is whispering to you.

Proper 27
Pentecost 25
Ordinary Time 32
Haggai 1:15b — 2:9

The Pastor Who Created A Monster

As Pastor Jenkins walked through the church fellowship hall he could not help overhearing part of a conversation between two members of his congregation. What he heard troubled him.

The members were standing in front of the big thermometer sign that the building committee had made. Five years ago the church had begun a fund campaign for a new sanctuary. The building committee had painted a big thermometer on a four-by-ten-foot sheet of plywood. The measurement markings on the thermometer were labeled, not in degrees, but in dollars. Each week the building committee chairman colored in the thermometer to correspond to the amount that had been given to the building fund to date. When the thermometer was finally colored in all the way to the top, that would indicate that they had enough money to build the new sanctuary.

Every time Pastor Jenkins passed the sign it reminded him that they were far behind their original timetable. The hope had been to have *all* the funds gathered within two years. Now, over twice the amount of time had passed, but the thermometer indicated that the congregation was only about half way to having enough money to build.

Pastor Jenkins had overheard two of the most active members of his church talking about the fund campaign for the new building. One member was commenting to the other how wonderful it was that so much money had been collected. She seemed very satisfied with the progress. She seemed totally oblivious of the fact that the congregation was nowhere *near* its goal. She was looking contentedly at the bottom half of the thermometer — the part that was all colored in. She did not even seem to notice the top half of the sign at all. She was not looking toward the *goal!* The other member did at least acknowledge the goal, but she did so with pessimism. She noted that, at the rate the congregation was going, they would never get a new sanctuary. She said they were trying to do too much, that it was impossible. Pastor Jenkins groaned inside at the comments he heard from both of the members. He decided to himself that something had to be done and that it was probably up to him.

As he prepared for his sermon for the next Sunday he tried to think of what he could say that would help people to catch a vision of the goal as well as what he could say to provide encouragement so that the members of the church would feel they could reach the goal. He finally decided upon what he thought was the perfect sermon text — the book of Haggai. When the church members came to worship the next Sunday, the sign in front of the church that announced the coming sermon read: "You Can Reach Your Goal — God Is With You!" The sign indicated that the sermon text was going to be Haggai 2:4.

When it came time for the sermon, the people watched as the pastor had two of the ushers bring the big thermometer sign from the fellowship hall and place it right next to the pulpit. Pastor Jenkins began his sermon by giving the people a little background on the prophet Haggai. He told them how the Jerusalem temple had been destroyed by the Babylonians and many of the Jews had been forced to leave their homeland to go and live in Babylon. Then, after a number of years, the Babylonians were overthrown by the Persians. Once the Persians were in control of things, Cyrus, the king of Persia, not only published a decree allowing the captive Jews to return home, but he also encouraged them to rebuild the Jerusalem temple on its original site. It was great news for the people. That was exactly what they had been longing to do.

The exiled Jews returned to Jerusalem and began work on the temple immediately. Within the first year they cleared away much of the rubble and began work on the foundation for a restored temple. But after that first year, for a variety of reasons, progress on the project slowed down a great deal and finally came to a complete stop.

Fifteen years later, the prophet Haggai confronted the people of Jerusalem and their leaders. The book of Haggai is a record of what went on. Haggai told them that it was time for them to finish what they had begun. He encouraged them to finish rebuilding the temple. More than that, he told them not just to get something built, but to build a temple that would be even more splendid than the glorious temple of Solomon, the temple that had been destroyed. What the prophet was doing was setting a clear *goal* in front of the people.

At this point, Pastor Jenkins reached down behind the pulpit and brought out a sign that he had made. It was a square of cardboard on which he had printed two words in large, bold letters. The sign said: "THE GOAL." Without saying a word, he moved out of the pulpit, stepped up on a chair so that he could reach the top of the building committee's sign and taped the words, "THE GOAL," to the very top of the thermometer.

Standing on the chair, with his chair by the top of the thermometer, Pastor Jenkins sensed that he had everyone's attention. He paused for a moment, for dramatic effect, and then he said, "The goal for the Jews in Jerusalem was to build a splendid temple. Our goal is to build a splendid new sanctuary."

He had not planned to do so, but he decided to remain standing on the chair rather than return to the pulpit. He was pretty sure he had everyone's attention. He did not want to break the momentum. He said, "The Jews of Haggai's time thought the goal before them was unrealistic — far more than they could ever possibly accomplish. Times were bad for the people. The economy was terrible. There had been drought and crop failures. Many of the people were living in poverty. How were they going to come up with the needed resources to build this splendid temple? Negative thinking ran rampant among the Jews!"

Pastor Jenkins' voice grew excited. Standing on the chair he found himself preaching with more passion than usual. He continued, "Then Haggai spoke an important word on behalf of God. The prophet told the people *how* they would accomplish the goal in front of them. Even though the goal seemed difficult or impossible to the people, the prophet now came with a word of God telling them why they should not sit on their hands — why they should move from apathy to action. People who thought that the goal before them was unreasonable and utterly impossible heard *this* word of the Lord spoken directly to them: 'Take courage, all you people ... for I am *with* you, says the Lord of hosts' (Haggai 2:4)."

After another long pause, Pastor Jenkins ended the sermon by saying simply, "You can reach your goal — God is with you." He stepped down from the chair and announced that in addition to the regular offering, a special offering for the building fund would be received.

Later that afternoon, the chairman of the building committee called the pastor and told him that they had counted the special offering and there had been a "very *good* response" to the sermon. That was Sunday afternoon. As the week continued, Pastor Jenkins began to discover that people were responding to the sermon in other ways as well. However, he was not so sure that all the ways were necessarily "good."

The first person to talk to the pastor about the sermon was Bruce. Bruce was a successful 36-year-old businessman. Bruce said he had just come by to thank the pastor for Sunday's sermon. He said that he knew that the pastor was talking about the "goal" for the building program, but Bruce went on to say that when he saw the pastor's sign that said, "THE GOAL," it made Bruce think of a major goal in his own life. He told the pastor that he had set a personal goal for himself to be able to retire by the time he was 60. Bruce explained that his finances had been lagging the last couple of years and that he had begun to think that it would be impossible. He told the pastor that he had slid into some negative thinking. Bruce said that he began to tell himself that he couldn't do it. But then, Bruce smiled brightly at his pastor and said, "Your sermon got me back on track. I know that I *can* do it and God will be with me as I do. I have a whole new perspective on my goal," he said. "I just wanted to stop by and thank you personally."

Fifteen minutes later Pastor Jenkins got a visit from another member of his congregation. Hank was in his mid-50s. Hank shook the pastor's hand and said, "That was *some* sermon you preached on Sunday! It really got me to thinking. You were talking about the temple in Jerusalem being a pile of rubble. Well, that reminded me of my business that collapsed last year. Suddenly before I knew it, all my work and plans and hopes and dreams were destroyed. It was all just a pile of rubble. The logical goal in front of me, of course, was to start over and rebuild the whole thing. But, so far, I haven't done much about it. I realize now that I have been standing around looking at the rubble of what happened to me before. I keep looking at the rubble and I think, "Why try again? It could all crumble down a second time. During your sermon, your little sign brought everything into focus for me. I realized that I've got to keep my eyes on THE GOAL." Hank shook the pastor's hand again. "Thank you for helping me see that. I've got to think positive. I've got to have *courage*, like Haggai said. I built a business once. I can do it again!" Hank moved toward the door and then added one last thing, "Besides," he said, "God is with me. Right?"

In addition to the visits, Pastor Jenkins received phone calls thanking him for the sermon. A teenage girl told him that the sermon made her realize that her goal was to get the relationship with her boyfriend back together. She said that she had been ready to give up, but now, she was going to work toward her goal. She said that, in addition, it was good to know that God was with her. That was a comfort.

Another parishioner, a heavy set, middle-aged man, said that he had been trying to lose weight, but he had just about given up. The whole thing seemed impossible to him. That was before the sermon. He told Pastor Jenkins that, after the sermon, he went home and put a sheet of paper on his refrigerator. At the top of the sheet he wrote "THE GOAL" in big letters. Under those letters he wrote the number of pounds that he planned to lose. At the bottom of the sheet he wrote the verse that had been the text for Sunday, "I am with you says the Lord of hosts" (Haggai 2:4).

There were other calls and visits. It was by far the biggest response Pastor Jenkins had ever received from a sermon. Nevertheless, the members of his church would have probably been surprised if they could have seen his reaction to all the responses. He closed the door to his office. He sat down at his desk, put his head in his hands and moaned to himself, "What have I done? What have I done? I think I've created a monster!"

The next Sunday the sign in front of the church that announced the coming sermon read: "A Better Sermon Than Last Week's Sermon." The sermon text from the previous week had not changed. It still read: Haggai 2:4.

When they saw the sermon title, the people were very curious as to what their pastor had in mind. When it came time for the sermon, the people watched again as the ushers carried in the big thermometer sign and placed it next to the pulpit. The thermometer still had the cardboard sign that said "THE GOAL" at the top. The only difference from the week before was that the building committee chairman had colored in more on the thermometer to indicate the amount given in the special offering from the previous Sunday.

Pastor Jenkins stood in the pulpit and said, "Let me begin with an apology. I want to apologize to you for last week's sermon. I believe that part of what I said was wrong. I want to take back some things I said." There was an audible murmur that ran through the congregation.

Without saying another word, the pastor moved out of the pulpit, stepped on a chair, so that he could reach the top of the building committee's sign, and removed the words, "THE GOAL," from the top of the thermometer.

Silently, he stepped down from the chair and walked to the cross behind the altar. Pastor Jenkins reached up and taped the words to the cross. He then walked back to the pulpit, reached down behind it and brought out three more cardboard signs exactly like the one he had just taped to the cross. He taped one to the baptismal font; he taped one to the altar that held the bread and wine for the eucharist; and he taped the last one to the large Bible that stood on the reading stand.

Pastor Jenkins turned to the people and said, "I got confused last week and I think I may have led some of you into confusion as well. The building project is not the goal of our life together as a congregation. To build a new sanctuary is certainly a good thing and an important thing to do. I believe that it is a God-pleasing thing. Work, family, personal achievement — these are all good things, but they are not the goal of our lives." Pastor Jenkins looked over the congregation and sensed that he had everyone's attention. He said, "God is the goal."

He continued, "The central point of the Haggai text is not that God is with us in what we do (although that *is* a point!). The central point is that the temple (work, success, family, and so forth) is not the goal of our life — God is the goal! When our lives become so much individual and corporate rubble, when all our hopes and dreams and plans have been turned into so much garbage or have been made superficial and narrow and mundane, it is not our "boot-strap, positive thinking" that will turn us into abundant, visionary people. Rather, it is our reliance on a faithful, present God. Our future does not depend on our successful doing and dreaming; our future depends on our faithful, present God."

The pastor stopped and looked into the eyes of the people in front of him. He wondered if they understood what he was trying to say. He continued, "You see, it is not a matter of our selecting a goal and then saying, 'Oh, by the way, isn't it nice that God is with us in this.' No, it is a matter of our first realizing that God is with us — period. That is the Christian faith. That is the goal! God is with us in the crucified Christ who comes to us in the holy Word and the sacraments. The goal is to meet God there. We come to worship and, by the grace of God, we experience a God who is with us.

"Oh yes, I am aware that our lives involve a Monday morning after our Sunday worship. I know that our lives are also filled with doing things. Our lives are filled with projects and that which we call goals. We make plans to build new buildings and we organize fund campaigns and we establish countless other projects in the life of a congregation and in our individual lives. But we need to be very careful. We need to remember that these other things are never THE GOAL. They are always our response to THE GOAL. They are our responses to the gift of God's presence in our lives.

"This is not to say that the various projects in our lives are unimportant. Quite the opposite. They are very important. They can be the way we live out our faith. They are our *response* to the phenomenal grace and empowering that we experience in God. We should treat them as nothing *less* than that — and, what I am trying to say to you today, we should treat them as nothing *more*." Pastor Jenkins paused and then said again, "We should treat them as nothing *more*."

With that, Pastor Jenkins said, "Amen." He then sat down and gave the people some time to think about what they had heard.

That is probably a good plan for this preacher to follow as well.

Amen.

Proper 28
Pentecost 26
Ordinary Time 33
Isaiah 65:17-25

Breaking Silence

Eight-year-old Robin could not believe it was happening! He had disobeyed his parents, but they had not yelled at him at all. In fact, they had not even said a single word to him. Robin truly could not believe it was happening! He thought to himself, "This is great!"

Since neither his mom or dad had said anything, and since it didn't look like they were planning to, Robin ran outside to play. After he had been playing for quite a while he noticed that it was starting to get dark. Robin also became aware that he was getting pretty hungry. He wondered why his parents hadn't called him in for supper yet. Robin went in the house and walked into the kitchen. To his surprise, he saw that his parents had already eaten dinner. His mom was putting some leftovers in the refrigerator and his dad was beginning to wash the dishes.

"I didn't hear you call me for supper," Robin said. Robin's father had his back to him at the sink and his mother was bent over arranging some things on the bottom shelf of the refrigerator. Neither of them said anything.

"Mom? Dad?" Robin said, "Why didn't you call me for supper?" Neither of his parents seemed to hear his question. At least, neither of them responded to him.

Robin watched in disbelief as his parents calmly completed their cleaning up chores. All the while they acted as if Robin was not even in the room. "Mom! Dad!" Robin yelled, "Why won't you answer me?" No matter how many times he asked them and no matter how loudly he shouted his questions at them, their answer was always the same — silence.

When Robin's parents had finished cleaning things up, they both walked into the family room leaving Robin in the kitchen by himself. Robin did not know what to think. Robin could not believe it was happening. He wished now that his parents *would* yell at him. Even that would be better than not talking to him at all.

Robin went to the refrigerator, got out some of the leftovers and sat at the kitchen table to eat his supper by himself. Even though he had been very hungry, the food did not make Robin feel better. His empty stomach was getting filled up, but a different kind of emptiness was sweeping over him. He was amazed at how alone he felt sitting in his own kitchen.

Robin went into the family room where his parents were watching television. Robin said in a loud voice, "Mom! Dad! Please! Please stop it! Why won't you talk to me? I'm sorry that I disobeyed you, but please stop doing this. I want you to talk to me!"

Robin's parents just kept watching the television. Neither of them said a word. Robin ran to the television and turned it off. He stood in front of the television set and faced his parents. "This isn't funny anymore!" he said. "You're scaring me! I need you to talk to me! Say something! Yell at me! Anything!"

Robin's father picked up the newspaper and his mother began reading a magazine. Robin began to cry. He stood in front of the television set for a long time with tears streaming down his face. Through his sobs he cried, "I can't believe this is happening! Please talk to me. Please. I need for you to talk to me. Please. Please!" The only sound that Robin heard from his parents was the sound of an occasional page turning. Otherwise, there was nothing but silence. Robin felt utterly alone surrounded by a complete, agonizing silence.

It was a silence that made Robin hurt inside. After a while his tears stopped. The silence was filling Robin with an ache that was too deep for tears. The dreadful silence of his parents was slowly breaking him. Their silence was pushing him deep into a terrifying loneliness. As steadily as the tick of a clock that echoed through the quiet house, the parents' silence was breaking the boy. It was pushing him into a deep despair. The silence was breaking him. It was pushing him to the depth of despair and toward danger.

Robin walked through the silent house into his father's bedroom. From a bedside stand Robin took out a pistol, raised it to his head and pulled the trigger.

The sound of the gun going off made Robin open his eyes with a start. He was sitting up in bed and he was shaking all over. He had had a *terrible* nightmare!

I admit that this is a pretty gruesome story. I suspect that some might even question whether it is perhaps too gruesome to be part of a sermon. Even so, I risked telling it because I wanted us to try to get a feeling of what it must have been like for the people described in the last chapters of the book of Isaiah. Theirs was a nightmare like Robin's nightmare. The only difference was, for them, it was real. It was a living nightmare.

The writer of the last chapters of Isaiah describes a painful situation for the children of Israel. There is some disagreement among biblical scholars as to whether the prophet is writing while the people are still in exile in Babylon or whether they have already returned home where they have encountered new problems. Actually, the confusion over their location really doesn't matter that much. Wherever they are, the prophet presents their dilemma with great clarity. The people are in despair because of their relationship with their heavenly parent — or, it would be more correct to say, their lack of a relationship.

Chapters 63 and 64 of Isaiah are a prayer to God. It is a lament prayer, a prayer of despair. The people believe that God has turned away from them. The words of the lament that the prophet writes are born out of the people's agony and travail. They believe that God's back is now turned to them. In their prayer of despair they admit that they have disobeyed God. They cry out to God that they "have sinned," that they are "unclean" and that their actions are like a "filthy cloth" (Isaiah 64:5-6).

The separation from God that their sin has caused leads them into deep despair because they know that there is not a thing *they* can do to heal the broken relationship. Their own sacred scriptures teach them that human beings cannot approach God. Their ancestors tried to do that on the tower of Babel and it ended in catastrophe (Genesis 11:1-9). Even someone like Moses had not been able to approach God. When Moses asked to see God's glory, God stuck Moses in the crack of a big rock and covered his eyes. God then passed by and Moses was allowed only to see God's back — certainly not God's face (Exodus 33:17-23). The mighty Creator God simply cannot be approached by sinful mortals. The people knew that they could cry out to God, but that there was no way for them to actually approach their heavenly parent. God, as parent, was in complete control of the relationship.

Knowing this, the people's lament ends with a pitiful question that cuts to the heart of their vulnerability, their fear and their loneliness. They ask, "Will you restrain yourself, O Lord? Will you keep silent, and punish us so severely?" (Isaiah 64:12). The people longed for a relationship with their God. They longed for communication with God. Divine silence was devastating. God's silence was devastating. God's silence would break them. In a prayer of despair they ask God, "Will you keep silent? Will you keep silent?"

Let's return to the story of Robin and his parents for a moment. When Robin woke from his nightmare his parents were sitting on his bed next to him. His mom was on one side and his dad on the other. Each of them had their arms around him. They had heard Robin talking in his sleep and had been trying to wake him from his bad dream.

In his nightmare Robin had dreamed that his parents had turned their backs on him and had broken him with silence. In the real world beyond his dreams, his parents already had their arms around him and were urging him to wake up, even while he was still experiencing his nightmare. When Robin did wake from his nightmare to the real world, he felt his parents' arms around him and heard their voice. They told him, "It's going to be all right, Robin. Don't worry. We're right here. You had a bad dream, but we're here with you and everything is okay."

As Robin moved from his nightmare to reality he allowed himself to relax into his parents' loving arms. He eagerly soaked in their comforting words. Their loving words broke the "silence" that he dreamed was breaking him.

With this scene before us, we look at the sermon text for today. It is from Isaiah 65, the chapter immediately following the lament chapters. It contains God's response to the people's prayer of despair. The people had prayed to God, asking, "Will you keep silent?" God's response reflects the very core of God's phenomenal grace toward the people. God says, "Before they call I will answer" (Isaiah 65:24). What a reply! "Before they call I will answer." God does not even wait for the people to ask. God breaks the silence that is breaking the people. God answers *before* they even ask!

When we disobey God — when our sin threatens to create a stony silence between us and our heavenly parent, it is God who breaks that silence. In his letter to the Romans Paul says, "God proves his love for us in that while we still were sinners Christ died for us" (Romans 5:8). Even before you ask, God breaks the silence and speaks a message of love and forgiveness through Jesus Christ. Even before you ask, God has already answered by wrapping you totally in love and acceptance. God's answer has already come to you in the complete forgiveness of all your sin.

By nature of our sinfulness we share the nightmare that plagued Robin and the children of Israel. The fear of a wall of silence separating us from our heavenly parent can fill us with dread and despair. It is a silence that can break us. What a joy that the silence that can break us has been broken by the God who answers even before we ask.

Thanksgiving Day
Deuteronomy 26:1-11

There's More To Thanksgiving

As Christian people we have come together to observe a time-honored American tradition. We have gathered for worship on Thanksgiving Day. Consequently, it may surprise you a little to learn that I plan to begin this sermon by telling you a story that could be labeled as downright un-American and blatantly non-Christian. Interestingly enough, it is possible that, if I had not said anything about it, you might have listened to this story and not have noticed anything unusual. In fact, even though I've now alerted you, it may still be difficult to detect what it is that's un-American and non-Christian about this story. So listen closely to see if you can figure it out. Are you ready? This is the story.

It was that time of year again. It was thanksgiving time. Farmers had finished the harvest. Businesses and schools had closed for the break. Not all, but most people had taken time off from work. After all, it *was* a national holiday. In keeping with tradition, there would be a special worship service, just like there was every year. In addition to the traveling and making special preparations, people would once again have the opportunity to worship.

This story is about three very religious people who lived in a rural community. It is a story about three people who chose to attend the annual thanksgiving worship service. Their names are Liz, Sam and Joe. They live in the country and each of them is involved in farming. However, each of them has his own view of what it means to be "thankful" for the harvest that is now out of the field and in the barns.

Liz does not actually do farm work herself. She is married to a farmer. Her husband farms a very large plot of land. This past year they did very well. It was a bumper crop for them. Liz and her husband are very happy about it. As faithful worshippers, they will tithe a full ten percent of everything that they received from the harvest. Considering the size of this year's crop, giving away ten percent means giving away a lot, but they do not mind. Even after giving so much in their offering, they will still have their remaining nine-tenths. It is enough to make them quite wealthy and, for that, they are thankful.

Sam also farms. He farms a much smaller area than Liz's husband does. For whatever reason, Sam's crop was not too good this year. Sam's barn is pretty small to begin with, but, even so, his harvest did not come close to filling it. Nonetheless, Sam is also faithful in giving his tithe every year. Discouraged as he is by how little he received from the land, he too plans to attend the special worship service. He will offer his tithe and give thanks for what crops he *does* have.

Finally there is Joe. Joe is a very young farmer. Some of his friends tease him about being more of a "nature lover" than a farmer. He sometimes goes out to his field and just looks at the earth. He stands in awe as he watches the miracle of planted seeds sprouting from the ground. As Joe brings his tithe to the special worship service, he does so conscious of the magical wonder that is bound up in the process of planting and harvesting.

Each of the three people approaches the worship service with a little different view of thankfulness. Liz is "happy thankful." Sam is "discouraged thankful." Joe is "awe-struck thankful." Yet, even though their viewpoints vary somewhat from each other, they each attend the thanksgiving worship service with the same thing in mind. Each goes to worship expecting it to be a time to offer God their thanks and their tithe. However, when they actually get to the worship, they discover that, this year, there's *more* going on — *much* more. The worship turns out not to be only a time for them to give their offering and speak a prayer of thanks. This year's worship now includes: "the creed" — and that changes everything. Attending *this* thanksgiving worship, Liz, Sam and Joe each discover that there is far *more* going on than they had realized. The end.

That's the story. What did you think? Was it as bad as I led you to expect, or did it actually seem like a fairly nice story to you? I would guess that for many people it probably sounded simply like a story about some pretty nice, fairly generous, "church-going" people. If you had a hard time figuring out what was so non-Christian and so un-American about it, allow me to let you in on the secret. You see, the "creed" that was said in the worship service was *not* the Apostles' Creed. Nor was it the Nicene Creed or the Athanasian Creed or any other Christian creed. In fact, Liz, Sam and Joe were not attending a *Christian* worship service at all. They were attending a harvest time, thanksgiving worship service all right, but it had *nothing* to do with our American Thanksgiving. The three worshippers in the story were not Americans. None of them lived anywhere near America. Neither did they worship in a time that was anywhere near the 20th century.

Although it may have sounded like it was a story about an American Thanksgiving worship service, much like the service we're having right now, it was actually a story about three Hebrew people attending the "feast of the first fruits" in Jerusalem, centuries *before* the birth of Christ. Such an event could not possibly be Christian and it certainly was not an American tradition. Nevertheless, the 26th chapter of Deuteronomy, the chapter which prescribes the worship for this ancient Hebrew festival, is the appointed Old Testament lesson which is to be read as we gather for *our* Thanksgiving Day worship. What, we might ask, could this text possibly have to say to our situation?

The "feast of first fruits," described by our Deuteronomy text, is also called by other names in scripture. It is sometimes called "the feast of harvest," and sometimes "the feast of weeks." The date of the festival was set by counting seven weeks from the time the sickle was put to the standing grain (Deuteronomy 16:9). Since it was celebrated on the 50th day after the beginning of the harvest, it was later given the name "Pentecost," since the Greek word *pentacosta* means 50. It is the same harvest festival that was taking place when the Holy Spirit came to the disciples and others in the second chapter of the book of Acts. But we're getting ahead of ourselves.

The story with which I began this sermon is a story about people attending this "feast of the first fruits." Liz, Sam and Joe are just nicknames I gave to worshippers who would probably have gone by the longer Hebrew names of Elizabeth, Samuel and Joseph. The particular characters, along with their scenarios, are just something I made up for the story, but the worship service I described them attending was not "made up."

After the ancient Hebrews finished the harvest each year, they took off work and traveled to Jerusalem to give a tithe of their crops. The Bible says the thanksgiving ceremony consisted of putting the first fruits of one's harvest in a basket and going to the central sanctuary to offer it before Yahweh. Once that was done, this ancient agricultural ceremony of first fruits was ended. Or we should probably say, that is how it worked each year until the writer of Deuteronomy announced to the people that now there was to be something *more* involved in the ceremony. The "something more" was a creed that the people were to memorize and repeat in the priest's hearing when the first fruits were offered. This creed, this statement of belief, consisted of a brief history of what God had done for them.

What is happening in our text is that the writer of Deuteronomy is taking a perfectly fine ceremony of thanksgiving, and is saying to the people: "There's more!" The message to the people is that now the harvest festival is to be not only about giving thanks for material things. It is also to be a time for remembering who God is. And there's even *more*. It is also to be a time to discover who they themselves are as a people in relationship with this God. It turns out that the writer of Deuteronomy intends for the whole thing to be quite a bit more than just an expression of thankfulness for material blessings.

In our text we read how the writer of Deuteronomy tells the people to recite one of the most ancient of all creeds. It is a brief but dramatic history of what God had done for the people. It tells how God delivered the people from bondage in Egypt and how God later gave them the promised land (Deuteronomy 26:5-9).

When we read this creed carefully we discover that the word choices used in the creed are very significant. The creed begins, "A wandering Aramean (i.e. Jacob) was my ancestor." It starts by the speaker looking back into the past from their vantage point in the present, but as the creed continues the speaker chooses words that eliminate the distance between the past and the present. When talking about their ancestors' time of bondage, the worshipper does *not* say, "When the Egyptians treated *them* harshly and afflicted *them* ..." Instead, the worshipper says, "When the Egyptians treated *us* harshly and afflicted *us* ..." (Deuteronomy 26:6). The creed moves from being simply a record of history about someone else to becoming the worshipper's *own* story. It is so much their own story that they speak as if they were actually present when it all happened. "The Lord brought *us* out of Egypt with a mighty hand" (Deuteronomy 26:8). It becomes more than just a creed. It becomes a personal creed, a statement of personal belief born out of a first-hand experience. The instruction to include this recitation of the history of God's mighty acts for the worshipper makes the first fruits ceremony quite a bit *more* than just an expression of thankfulness for material blessings.

And now, this ancient text, this set of instructions given to people living thousands of years ago, this set of instructions telling them how to properly observe the "feast of first fruits" in the Jerusalem temple, is *our* text for a contemporary

American Thanksgiving service. It's rather amazing when you think about it. Yet, as strange as it might seem at first, it is actually quite a wonderful text for American Christians to be reading on our national holiday of Thanksgiving. It is a good text for this occasion because it takes a perfectly fine holiday and says: There's more.

Let me first be very clear in saying that I believe that Thanksgiving Day in the USA is indeed a perfectly good holiday. It is good for us as a country to reflect on our national history. It is a good thing to teach our children about the pilgrims thanking God in a meal celebrating the harvest. It is good that people throughout the land are remembering and giving thanks for all God's blessings to them. Some, like Liz in the story, have received much and it is good for them to offer God their word of thanks. Others, like Sam , may be discouraged that they have less than their neighbor, but their words of thanks to God for what they *do* have are no less important. Even the smallest blessing is a gift which merits our thanks. This day can also serve as an occasion for us to pause, like Joe, and reflect on the wonder and miraculous glory that is a part of every gift that we experience in and through God's creation.

Thanksgiving Day is a perfectly good holiday for our country just as the "feast of first fruits" was a perfectly good holiday for the children of Israel. Because of that, the text from Deuteronomy 26 is a tremendous text for this day because it does for us exactly what it did for the Hebrew people centuries ago. It takes a perfectly fine holiday and says: There's more!

It may be non-American and pre-Christian, but this text, concerning a thanksgiving festival, can remind American Christians that today is not only a time to remember all God's material gifts to us. It is also a time to remember who God is and who we are as a people who have been brought into a relationship with that God. If this text does that for us, that is definitely quite a bit *more* than a simple nod of the head while saying grace before devouring a turkey dinner.

When Deuteronomy included the creed in the first fruits celebration is was including a powerful piece of history. Focusing on what God had *done*, in addition to merely thanking God for the gift of material blessings, enabled the people to perceive the much wider wealth of God's goodness toward them. Yes, a loving God *had* provided the miracle of growth and harvest so the people could eat and live, but there was more — much more. This same God had also delivered them from bondage in Egypt and had given them the freedom and prosperity of the promised land. The creeds of God's church in our time enable us also to perceive the wide wealth of God's goodness. We have been delivered from the bondage of sin and we have been given the peace and joy that comes to us in Christ.

The writer of Deuteronomy calls us to use our Thanksgiving Day worship as a time to acknowledge far more than merely our thankfulness for God's material blessings to us. It is a call to reflect on the full story of God's action in history. From our vantage point in time we know even more of the wonderful story of what God is up to in the world. The creeds of the Christian era speak of even more of God's saving action than the ancient creed recorded in our text. The creeds of God's church today acknowledge the glorious history of the Creator who brought us and all things into being; they acknowledge Jesus Christ who recreated us with the gift of new life and the forgiveness of our sins; and they acknowledge the Spirit, the "giver of life," who renews and sustains us through our baptism.

Even though the American story of the pilgrims' thankfulness to God for their first harvest is an important part of our Thanksgiving Day tradition, there is definitely more. The story of the first Thanksgiving is a fine and good story in our nation's history, but "the best" Thanksgiving story is the story of what God has done in the history of humankind. And the best part of "the best" story is that it is *our* story. It is a story that tells us "who" we are by telling us "whose" we are.

As American Christians and citizens of this country it is good for us to recall the history of the first Thanksgiving Day observed by early American settlers and it is good to speak our own thankfulness to God for all the blessings we enjoy in this land. It is good for us to give thanks whether we feel we have been given a lot or a little. But there's more. As citizens of God's kingdom we also recall the history of God's deliverance to the people of the past and to us. It is in the record of God's loving acts as Creator, Christ and Spirit that we experience the much wider wealth of God's goodness. In the marvelous history of God's loving action, which is recorded in the church's creeds of today, we remember the culminating act of God's love for us in the story of Jesus Christ. *"His* story is the climax of all "history." "His story" is the best history — for Americans and for everyone.

Christ The King
Jeremiah 23:1-6

Close Quarters With A King

It was quite unusual for Susan to do something so frivolous. Perhaps it was the combination of depression and stress that prompted her to take a break from her daily responsibilities. There was quite a bit of tension in Susan's relationship with her husband. Also her teenage children seemed to have become almost completely out of her control. She felt frustrated and helpless. She felt that she *needed* something. In fact, when she tried to think of a word to describe how she was feeling, that was the word that came to mind: "needy." Almost as an act of desperation, she got in her car and began driving to a nearby town. There she bought herself a nice lunch. After lunch she decided to drive over to a seminary campus located in the town. It was perhaps an odd place to spend the afternoon, but a friend from church had told her that they gave tours each afternoon. Apparently the buildings on the campus had some very impressive mosaics.

Susan joined a tour and enjoyed it a great deal. Her guide directed the group to what he told them was the largest mosaic on the campus. Standing in front of the artwork Susan looked up at a picture of Christ as a king seated on a throne. The mosaic was *very* large — over 20 feet tall. Christ sat in royal splendor. He wore a kingly robe. At his feet was a stylized half moon and seven stars (stylized in the form of molecular structures). Christ was pictured as king of the whole creation — down to the very atoms. In his right hand he held the orb of the world. He was seated on a golden throne and he was crowned with an ornate crown.

Susan knew that the Bible talked about Christ as a king, but as she looked up at the figure before her she thought it was odd that she had never before seen an artistic portrayal of Christ in the role of a king. She became aware that in her mind she had almost always envisioned Jesus as a shepherd or a teacher or a servant or maybe a healer. A young child in the tour group spoke Susan's thoughts out loud. He said, "Gee, this is the first time I ever *really* thought of him as a king." Susan considered how her previous ways of imagining Christ had never even come close to acknowledging the kind of power she sensed looking at this image. An elderly man in the group whispered aloud to no one in particular, "If you're looking for a king who can take care of you, it sure looks like this is someone who could do the job."

As Susan looked up at the figure she took a very deep breath. She began to feel a slight easing of her depression and stress — an easing of her "neediness." She thought to herself, "Yes, it's true. In Christ we have a king who will meet all our needs."

Standing before the mosaic each of the visitors felt as if there were an overwhelming power emanating from this king. Coupled with this power was a sense of royal splendor that seemed to call for a measure of regal distance. Everyone found themselves wanting to move back a bit from the king before them, but they couldn't. For, you see, this mosaic was not on the wall of a large open room. It was on the wall of a hallway. There was a glass wall about ten to 12 feet directly opposite this picture of Christ on the throne. The visitors stood with their backs pressed against the glass. A passerby observing the group might have thought that they were just trying to move back in order to visually take in the whole work of art. Certainly that was part of the reason for trying to back up, but only part. The major reason for their backing up was really quite straightforward. Common, ordinary people simply do not stand at close quarters with a king — at least not comfortably.

Susan stood looking up at the bigger-than-life king while her own back was pressed against the glass wall. Again she thought to herself, "Yes, in Christ we have a king who will meet all our needs." Then something deep within her, something rumbling around in the midst of her unmet needs, caused her to add, "or will he?"

I'm going to ask you to please set this scene aside in your mind for a moment. We will come back to Susan in just a bit, but first let's go back over 2,500 years to a time when the image of a king could have been a very prevalent image in most people's minds.

During this period of time there was a nation of people who did not have a king but who desperately wanted one. They wanted someone who would hold a position of great power so that he could use that power to meet the needs of all the people in the nation. This ancient nation asked their God to raise up a king for them. They wanted someone who would be set apart and above them as royalty. They wanted a king who would sit over them to rule in strength. One who would lead in making their nation great. And the name of that nation, as you have probably guessed, was Israel.

Finally, after they had begged and begged for it, Yahweh allowed Israel to have a king. Over time, they had a long line of kings. However, the kings were a surprise to the people — not a pleasant surprise. The people of Israel, for their part, had honored their kings by giving them a proper royal distance and power. In return they expected the kings to use their power to meet the nation's needs and care for them as a shepherd cares for the sheep. To Israel's dismay, most of her kings were better endured than honored. The kings certainly distanced themselves from the people and they most definitely had power. The problem was that they often used their power against the people. The prophet Jeremiah refers to the problem in today's Old Testament lesson, "Thus says the Lord, the

God of Israel, concerning the shepherds who shepherd my people: It is you who have scattered my flock, and have driven them away" (Jeremiah 23:2). Israel's kings had not cared for the needs of the people. The people felt frustrated and helpless. Their stress and depression levels were very high.

It was a "needy" time for the people. Fortunately, Jeremiah also brings some pretty amazing good news from Yahweh.

Jeremiah tells the people that Yahweh will "raise up shepherds over them who will shepherd them" and the people will no longer need to "fear any longer, or be dismayed" (v. 4). The prophet proclaims that God will raise up a messianic king, a "righteous Branch," a true shoot from the stock of King David. This Old Testament passage is like a drum roll that precedes a spectacular event. The words of this text are like the rumbling on some giant snare drum that builds anticipation as Jeremiah's prophecy points to the coming of the one who will be a truly amazing king for Israel in comparison to what she's had to this point. This promised king will be a normal king in that he will possess power and everyone will bow before him giving him proper regal distance. But, the prophet says, "He shall reign as king and deal wisely, and shall execute justice and righteousness in the land. In his days Judah will be saved and Israel will live in safety" (vv. 5-6).

The words rumble in the ears of the people of Israel. The promise of such a king crescendos in the hearts and hope of the people for many years. Finally it comes to a tremendous climax on a day we now call Christmas. Jesus the Christ, the Anointed One, is born. Finally comes the king who, the gospel writer says, "will be great, and will be called the Son of the Most High, and the Lord God will give to him the throne of his ancestor David. He will reign over the house of Jacob forever, and of his kingdom there will be no end" (Luke 1:32-33). What a description! What power! What regal distance this king deserves! Certainly a drum roll that lasted hundreds of years was not too much of a fanfare to announce this awesome King of kings! Oh, how Israel had longed for the day when it could be said, "In the Anointed One, in the

Christ we have a king who will finally meet all our needs." Yes indeed. "In Christ we have a king who meets all our needs."

Now let's return again to Susan. She was staring at the wall in front of her where Jesus sat upon his throne in dazzling splendor. Her back was pressed against the glass behind her as she tried to give regal distance to this king. She felt uncomfortable being at such close quarters with this king. Yet, at the same time, Susan was glad to be in the presence of this artwork and all that it symbolized for her. What power!

She thought to herself, "In Christ we have a king who will meet all our needs." But then she paused again. "Or will he?" There was a part of her that felt like she should be singing the "Hallelujah Chorus" from Handel's *Messiah,* "The Lord God Omnipotent reigneth. Hallelujah. Hallelujah." To the amazement of all the world, the ancient hope had come true. And now the Christ had come. He rules as king of truth and justice. God is ultimately in control — on the throne! "Hallelujah. Hallelujah."

As a Christian Susan had been taught that all this was true, and yet questions crept into her mind. What about the hungry people in the world? What about people who were victims to crime and oppression? What about the places in the world where justice does *not* prevail? What about the places in her own country where that happens?

Susan thought about her family. The reason she had taken the day off was that she was feeling overwhelmed with problems. She felt as if her marriage and family were falling apart. She also thought about all the times she had sat in front of the television watching the evening news. Sometimes it seemed to her that the whole world was falling apart. As she stared at the mosaic she thought to herself, "All right, Christ is King. That is true. But what does his reign really amount to? How does his reign bring peace to my family? How is Christ in actuality the ruler of kings on this earth? Where is Christ's reign? Where is his royal judgment as king over the little wrongs and giant atrocities?"

Susan reflected again on the fact that she had never seriously envisioned Jesus in the role of king before that day. Was it possibly because the only place where he is historically called "king" and where the name sticks is in the title over the place where he died. There on the cross he is not a king of power and regal distance. There on the cross he is not king over the insignificant and weak of the world. There he is himself insignificant and weak. What kind of king is that? There on the cross he is himself among the hungry and oppressed weak and the abused and the forgotten and the war-ravaged and the heaped-up dead. Susan thought to herself, "What kind of a king is that?" As the tour guide moved them to the next building she thought to herself, "What kind of a king is that?"

That was Susan's question, "What kind of a king is that?" Maybe in some ways that is our question too. Maybe we usually do not think of Jesus in terms of a king at all. I suspect that many of us, like Susan, usually think of Jesus primarily as shepherd or teacher or servant or healer. But today it is hard to avoid this image. Today the historical tradition of the church brings the role of king to our attention. Today, the last Sunday in the church year, is Christ The King Sunday. The Christian church is making a bold assertion here. Around the world on this day Christians are acknowledging, in fact celebrating, that Christ is the king. Given what is actually happening around the world, some people no doubt think this is an amazing thing for the church to say — much less celebrate.

Now, most Christians are probably quick to agree that this assertion is certainly true. But, if we are honest, we may have to admit that there is a bit of embarrassment or incredulity for us in this truth. When we have said that this Jesus is all the fulfillment of the ancient hope of Jeremiah's day for a just and true king, then we must look at him again. And when we look again we know that what Susan thought as she stood before the massive picture of Jesus is also correct. He is no traditional king and never was. No, instead of being a king he was led to a cross, and the only kingship he knew was a cruel mocking before his death and a mocking title put up over his agony.

And he, of course, is not the Son of Man of Jewish expectation, appearing with marvelous angels surrounding him and exercising an authority to which all are immediately obedient. Jesus is not that. No angels hover around his cross, even though Christian art of the Middle Ages may have imagined them there. All nations are not gathered before him. All those people are not immediately obedient to his word.

No, finally he is simply there in the midst of the agony of many other people of the world. He is there, hidden away in the midst of all the suffering and dying and oppressed ones. And all that there is left of him, all that seems to remain, is just his prayer: "Father, forgive them," and the more agonizing prayer, "My God, why have you forsaken me?" He is reduced finally to that. Not a king, not the Son of Man, not the center of the angels, not the heart of the reigning and the ruling in the universe. He is reduced simply to his prayer, to waiting for God and his kingdom, waiting and crying out for God even in the midst of his death.

And there, in the midst of his death, he is identified with the ones whom he calls his sisters and brothers. He is hungry with the hungry, thirsty with the thirsty, a stranger outside the camp with the strangers, naked with the naked, sick unto death with the sick, imprisoned and mocked with the prisoners. That is where he is. He is clearly in the company of those for whom stress and depression levels are high.

He is there. And the amazing thing about the Christian faith is that it confesses that it is *there* that he rules! Christians have always understood the title over his cross as ironically true. The "needy" of this world have always experienced close quarters with this king. Common, ordinary people can feel quite comfortable being close to this king. Stressed and depressed people like Susan, and like you and me, can experience close quarters with this King of kings because he was chosen to be among us in our need.

Jeremiah's drum roll encouraged the people to anticipate a pretty amazing kind of kingdom — "justice and righteousness in the land." Was it an accurate prophecy? Did the most amazing monarch of all time appear? The present kingdom in which we find ourselves may not look all that amazing at times. It is possible that when you look around you will see a considerable amount of injustice and a good number of unmet needs on the part of others and yourself. Yet, perhaps the secret is to look not only at the kingdom, but at the king. Actually, the promised messiah turned out to be a more amazing king than anyone could have imagined. Granted, this king has not promised to *meet* all our needs, but he does promise to meet us *in* our need.

Lectionary Preaching After Pentecost

The following index will aid the user of this book in matching the correct Sunday with the appropriate text during Pentecost. All texts in this book are from the series for Lesson One, Revised Common Lectionary. Lutheran and Roman Catholic designations indicate days comparable to Sundays on which Revised Common Lectionary Propers are used.

(Fixed dates do not pertain to Lutheran Lectionary)

Fixed Date Lectionaries *Revised Common and Roman Catholic*	**Lutheran Lectionary** *Lutheran*
The Day of Pentecost	The Day of Pentecost
The Holy Trinity	The Holy Trinity
May 29-June 4 — Proper 4, Ordinary Time 9	Pentecost 2
June 5-11 — Proper 5, Ordinary Time 10	Pentecost 3
June 12-18 — Proper 6, Ordinary Time 11	Pentecost 4
June 19-25 — Proper 7, Ordinary Time 12	Pentecost 5
June 26-July 2 — Proper 8, Ordinary Time 13	Pentecost 6
July 3-9 — Proper 9, Ordinary Time 14	Pentecost 7
July 10-16 — Proper 10, Ordinary Time 15	Pentecost 8
July 17-23 — Proper 11, Ordinary Time 16	Pentecost 9
July 24-30 — Proper 12, Ordinary Time 17	Pentecost 10
July 31-Aug. 6 — Proper 13, Ordinary Time 18	Pentecost 11
Aug. 7-13 — Proper 14, Ordinary Time 19	Pentecost 12
Aug. 14-20 — Proper 15, Ordinary Time 20	Pentecost 13
Aug. 21-27 — Proper 16, Ordinary Time 21	Pentecost 14
Aug. 28-Sept. 3 — Proper 17, Ordinary Time 22	Pentecost 15
Sept. 4-10 — Proper 18, Ordinary Time 23	Pentecost 16
Sept. 11-17 — Proper 19, Ordinary Time 24	Pentecost 17

Sept. 18-24 — Proper 20, Ordinary Time 25	Pentecost 18
Sept. 25-Oct. 1 — Proper 21, Ordinary Time 26	Pentecost 19
Oct. 2-8 — Proper 22, Ordinary Time 27	Pentecost 20
Oct. 9-15 — Proper 23, Ordinary Time 28	Pentecost 21
Oct. 16-22 — Proper 24, Ordinary Time 29	Pentecost 22
Oct. 23-29 — Proper 25, Ordinary Time 30	Pentecost 23
Oct. 30-Nov. 5 — Proper 26, Ordinary Time 31	Pentecost 24
Nov. 6-12 — Proper 27, Ordinary Time 32	Pentecost 25
Nov. 13-19 — Proper 28, Ordinary Time 33	Pentecost 26 Pentecost 27
Nov. 20-26 — Christ the King	Christ the King

Reformation Day (or last Sunday in October) is October 31 (Revised Common, Lutheran)

All Saints' Day (or first Sunday in November) is November 1 (Revised Common, Lutheran, Roman Catholic)

Books In This Cycle C Series

Gospel Set

When It Is Dark Enough
Sermons For Advent, Christmas And Epiphany
Charles H. Bayer

Walking To ... Walking With ... Walking Through
Sermons For Lent And Easter
Glenn E. Ludwig

The Divine Advocacy
Sermons For Pentecost (First Third)
Maurice A. Fetty

Troubled Journey
Sermons For Pentecost (Middle Third)
John Lynch

Extraordinary Faith For Ordinary Time
Sermons For Pentecost (Last Third)
Larry Kalajainen

First Lesson Set

The Days Are Surely Coming
Sermons For Advent, Christmas And Epiphany
Robert A. Hausman

Turning Obstacles Into Opportunities
Sermons For Lent And Easter
Rodney Thomas Smothers

Grapes Of Wrath Or Grace?
Sermons For Pentecost (First Third)
Barbara Brokhoff

Summer Fruit
Sermons For Pentecost (Middle Third)
Richard L. Sheffield

Stepping Inside The Story
Sermons For Pentecost (Last Third)
Thomas G. Rogers

www.ingramcontent.com/pod-product-compliance
Lightning Source LLC
Chambersburg PA
CBHW061459040426
42450CB00008B/1418